Understanding and Enriching Problem Solving in Primary Mathematics

CRITICAL TEACHING

You might also like the following books from Critical Publishing.

Teaching Systematic Synthetic Phonics and Early English
By Jonathan Glazzard and Jane Stokoe
978-1-909330-09-2 In print

Primary School Placements: A Critical Guide to Outstanding Teaching
Catriona Robinson, Branwen Bingle and Colin Howard
978-1-909330-45-0 In print

Teaching and Learning Early Years Mathematics: Subject and Pedagogic Knowledge
Mary Briggs
978-1-909330-37-5 In print

Beyond Early Reading
Ed David Waugh and Sally Neaum
978-1-909330-41-2 In print

Inclusive Primary Teaching
Janet Goepel, Helen Childerhouse and Sheila Sharpe
978-1-909330-29-0 In print

Most of our titles are also available in a range of electronic formats. To order please go to our website www.criticalpublishing.com or contact our distributor, NBN International, 10 Thornbury Road, Plymouth PL6 7PP, telephone 01752 202301 or email orders@nbninternational.com.

Understanding and Enriching Problem Solving in Primary Mathematics

 Patrick Barmby, David Bolden
& Lynn Thompson

CRITICAL
TEACHING

First published in 2014 by Critical Publishing Ltd

British Library Cataloguing in Publication Data
A CIP record for this book is available from the British Library

ISBN: 978-1-909330-69-6

This book is also available in the following e-book formats:

MOBI ISBN: 978-1-909330-70-2
EPUB ISBN: 978-1-909330-71-9
Adobe e-reader ISBN: 978-1-909330-72-6

Cover and text design by Greensplash Limited
Project Management by Out of House Publishing
Printed and bound in Great Britain by Bell & Bain, Glasgow

Critical Publishing
152 Chester Road
Northwich
CW8 4AL
www.criticalpublishing.com

MIX
Paper from
responsible sources
FSC® C007785
www.fsc.org

Contents

Acknowledgements

The authors would like to thank the following for their kind permission to use Copyright material in this book.

The cartoon on page 12 is taken from the Department for Education and Employment's Challenges booklet, © Crown Copyright 2000, ISBN 0-19-312342-8, illustration by Graham Round.

A number of questions have been reproduced from original SATs papers. These are Crown copyright and are gratefully reproduced free of charge under the terms of the Open Government Licence.

Every effort has been made to trace copyright holders and to obtain their permission for the use of copyright material. The publisher and authors will gladly receive information enabling them to rectify any error or omission in subsequent editions.

Meet the authors

Patrick Barmby is a Lecturer in Primary Mathematics at Durham University and is the Programme Director for the BA Primary Education course at Durham. Patrick's area of research is in primary mathematics, with a particular focus on developing children's understanding in mathematics. He has also carried out research projects on developing teachers' knowledge in primary mathematics. For him, the best parts of teaching on the Primary Education degree at Durham University have been not only influencing student teachers' practice in primary mathematics, but also being influenced himself by the wealth of experiences and expertise from the classroom that students bring to the sessions.

David Bolden is a Lecturer in Mathematics Education at Durham University where he teaches on the BA Primary Education, PGCE Primary Education and MSc Mathematics Education courses. His research interests include creativity in mathematics and teacher epistemologies, particularly in relation to primary mathematics.

Lynn Thompson is an educational consultant and founder of North East School Support (NESS), supporting schools to raise standards and improve the teaching and learning of mathematics. She also teaches part time on the Primary BA and PGCE courses at Durham University.

1 Introduction

Key issues in this chapter

- This introductory chapter begins by outlining the reasons for writing this book and why we feel that it is important for teachers to be clear about the teaching and learning of problem solving.

- It sets out a short history of the ways in which problem solving has been conceived and incorporated into the different iterations of the primary curricula, and why this book is timely.

- Having justified 'why' we have written this book, the chapter outlines 'what' the book contains in terms of problem solving and 'how' we have approached the topic.

Introduction

This book is about problem solving in the primary mathematics classroom. We should state at the outset that we are acutely aware that there exist a number of very good books already published on the subject (for instance, Polya, 1957, Burton, 1984, and Mason, Burton & Stacey, 1985, to name just a few), but we think we have something to add. Reflecting upon the teaching, understanding and use of problem solving skills, we felt there was now a need for a complementary yet different style of book which would not only inform teachers, but would directly support their teaching in the classroom. This book is akin to a high-quality training course, a course that you can complete at your own leisure and that will undoubtedly improve pedagogical practice and impact upon children's understanding, engagement and achievement. This book is an amalgamation of previous and current research findings that will question your thinking and test your subject knowledge. It unpicks the problem-solving process in detail and discusses classroom implications that relate directly to the requirements of the national curriculum (DfE, 2013). We present chapters that ask questions like *What is the nature of a problem and of the problem solving process? What type of characteristics should genuine problems exhibit? And what does all this mean for the mathematics classroom, the child and the teacher?* Each chapter deals with a different part of the process as we view it and provides an up-to-date review of the research and theory relating to that particular aspect. In addition, each chapter also provides concrete pedagogical examples of those aspects in action in the primary classroom. We encourage current trainees, NQTs and established teachers to question their own practice in the light of what we discuss in this book. We acknowledge that developing and incorporating problem solving as we view it in the classroom is not always easy, but we think that the results will be worth the effort, both for the teacher and the child.

Why now?

Problem solving has always been viewed by many in the field of mathematics education to be at the very heart of mathematics. We think the book is particularly timely because problem solving now seems to be taking on greater importance in the eyes of policy makers, for whom this certainty has not always existed. For instance, the government's education watchdog, Ofsted, recently identified the planning and assessing of problem solving as an area of weakness in trainee teachers' practice and suggested this as an area for improvement (Ofsted, 2013). As a result, we are in a situation where there appears to be a large degree of consensus concerning the importance of problem solving in the teaching and learning of mathematics. It is now viewed as important by both academics and policy makers and we think this is encouraging. We hope this book will build on and further contribute to that consensus while also helping teachers to engage with the central ideas.

A short 30-year history of problem solving in the UK

The Cockroft report

It was the Cockroft report in the UK (Cockroft, 1982) which re-established problem solving at the heart of effective learning and teaching in mathematics, although many in the field of mathematics education had never swayed from that belief. The Cockroft report was commissioned by the UK government at a time when concerns were being raised that young children in primary schools were not developing the necessary mathematical skills and understanding and that teachers were relying too heavily on published schemes in their teaching. The report argued that *'the ability to solve problems is at the heart of mathematics'* (Cockcroft, 1982, p.249). It included in its list of recommendations that problem solving be better integrated into the primary mathematics curriculum, including more investigational work, and that mathematical knowledge be better applied to everyday situations.

The national curriculum

Although much good work continued in the following years, including the publication of influential books by Burton (1984) and Mason et al (1985) mentioned above, by the late 1980s there still existed a concern, predominantly but not exclusively in industry, that children in English schools were under-performing. The Conservative government at the time attempted to address that concern by adopting a 'back to basics' approach which set about prescribing what children should be taught and when. In the first iteration of this national curriculum in 1988–89 (DfES, 1989), problem solving was encapsulated in the term 'using and applying' mathematics. This was useful in that it seemed to distinguish between the learning of mathematical facts and skills, and the more important and overarching processes of applying those facts and skills in unfamiliar situations. These processes included enquiring, representing, reasoning, and communicating. However, although many were encouraged by this new emphasis on problem solving, the way in which using and applying was positioned within and among the other aspects of the curriculum, eg as a separate attainment target, seemed to suggest it was not conceived as a process that should be applied across all areas of mathematics. Moreover, assessment of children's progression – in all areas of mathematics – was to take the form of standardised tests, and high stakes tests at that, which were not and are not conducive to assessing children's problem-solving processes.

In a subsequent iteration of the national curriculum in 1999 (DfEE, 1999a), 'using and applying' was no longer to be seen as a separate entity but was now incorporated into each of the other aspects of the primary mathematics curriculum. At about the same time, the National Numeracy Strategy was introduced (DfEE, 1999b). This set out a framework for teaching mathematics across the primary age range and offered teachers a great deal of structure, including the three-part numeracy lesson. However, the emphasis was on calculating and number work and not on problem solving per se, which was seen by many as an 'add-on' and not something that was integral to everyday mathematics.

In 2003 the Labour government set out a new vision for primary education with the publication of Excellence and Enjoyment: A Strategy for Primary Schools (DfES, 2003). Although it emphasised that children should be enthused by mathematics, it mentioned creativity more than problem solving or 'using and applying'. The Primary National Strategy framework documents (DfES, 2006a; 2006b) re-emphasised the central importance of 'using and applying' by stating that it needed to be *embedded into the teaching and learning of mathematics*', that it *'become a regular part of children's work... [and that] ...problem solving should not be seen as a "Friday only" activity.'* (p.7). The Williams Review (DCSF, 2008) continued this closer examination of the mathematics curriculum, with a particular emphasis on provision in primary schools. It argued that the curriculum on offer was '*... by and large, well balanced'* but argued for *'an increased focus on the "use and application"* of mathematics' (p.4).

The Rose Review (DCSF, 2009) was commissioned by the then Labour government to examine the entire primary curriculum and its main aim was to suggest a provision that was fit for purpose as we moved into the twenty-first century. It advocated mathematical understanding as one of six main areas of study with, again, an emphasis on 'using and applying', but its recommendations came at the end of Labour's term of office and were quickly discarded by the incoming Conservative government. All this was happening at a time when Ofsted was reporting general findings that children observed during inspections often had the ability to perform written calculations but were not so good at applying that knowledge in unfamiliar and/or real-life situations. The report, Mathematics: Understanding the Score (Ofsted, 2008), painted a gloomy picture in terms of children's ability to use and apply their mathematics knowledge:

> *Too often, pupils are expected to remember methods, rules and facts without grasping the underpinning concepts, making connections with earlier learning and other topics, and making sense of the mathematics so that they can use it independently. The nature of teaching and assessment, as well as the interpretation of the mathematics curriculum, often combine to leave pupils ill equipped to use and apply mathematics. Pupils rarely investigate open-ended problems which might offer them opportunities to choose which approach to adopt or to reason and generalise.*
>
> (Ofsted, 2008, p.5)

In light of its findings, the report went on to recommend that separate reporting of children's attainment in the area of *'using and applying mathematics'* be reintroduced as part of the statutory teacher assessments at the end of each key stage.

The present day

The advent of the new national curriculum (DfE, 2013) brings us to the present day. Here we see that using and applying is again regarded as an integral part of the curriculum and that children are expected to *'... solve problems by applying their mathematics to a variety of routine and non-routine problems with increasing sophistication, including breaking down problems into a series of simpler steps and persevering in seeking solutions.'* (p.3).

Much good work was conducted by those in the field of mathematics education during this time (eg NRICH) but the history of problem solving over the last 30 years is perhaps best summed up by Burkart and Bell (2007) in their useful historical account. They write that the history of problem solving in the UK *'... illustrates the way policy decisions, taken on plausible grounds by people with good intentions but limited understanding, frequently have unintended consequences that undermine the very goals they seek to advance'* (p.401). Consequently, the results in the classroom have, up until now, been patchy at best.

Primary teachers' experiences with problem solving

As the following chapters will illustrate, problem solving requires the solver to use a number of what we might call *'higher level skills'* (Burkart and Bell, 2007: p.395), eg patience, resilience, logical reasoning and a range of meta-cognitive skills, and so it is perhaps not surprising that primary teachers, who are often not specialists in any particular subject domain, have not always felt comfortable with delivering this aspect of the curriculum. Our own research (Bolden, Harries and Newton, 2010), and the research of others, shows that primary teachers often view mathematics as an unchanging set body of knowledge to be taught and learned. They regard the primary aim of lessons as the learning of specific procedures, sometimes by rote, and ultimately the search for the one, and only one, right answer. Primary teachers may have sound mathematical subject knowledge in this respect but it can often be lacking in conceptual knowledge, that is the type of knowledge which allows them to make links between what appear to be disparate areas of mathematics, ie to understand. We do not wish to suggest that rote learning is not important, it can be very useful in the right context, but we do wish to suggest that true problem solving requires a broader and richer range of skills.

There is sometimes great pressure on teachers to cover the content in the curriculum (Bolden and Newton, 2008) and this does not help them to develop rich problems with which children can explore mathematics. Creating rich problems and engaging in real problem solving takes time – both on the part of the teachers and the children – and the current and past curricula have left teachers feeling there is insufficient time and space for this to happen successfully.

How this book is organised

Given teachers' experiences with problem solving, this book sets out to clarify exactly what problem solving is, the processes involved in problem solving (including thinking and learning processes by children), and how problem solving and the variety of related processes can be incorporated into the mathematics classroom. The approach we have taken on problem solving in this book is to take a primary classroom perspective, rather than considering it from a more 'advanced' perspective related to degree, A-level or even secondary mathematics. The main reason for this is to show that, even with younger children, you can incorporate problem-solving approaches in your teaching. However, this does not mean that this book is relevant to primary teachers only. In fact, in putting forward our arguments throughout the book, we draw on research on problem solving across the age range of schooling. You might adapt the examples given for the children that you work with, but the important thing that we want you to take from this book is this clearer view of problem solving.

Therefore, in Chapter 2, the first thing we look at is what problem solving is. In doing so, we question what a 'problem' is, and then explore suggestions from research and practice on how we might suggest children tackle these problems, thereby clarifying the problem solving process. You will see from our discussions regarding this process that 'representing' the problem situation, and the mathematical reasoning or thinking involved, are crucial aspects of this process. Therefore, in Chapter 3, we examine this issue of representing problems, and in Chapter 4, we examine the process of reasoning and how we reason with problems. Strongly related to this issue of reasoning is the creative process involved in problem solving, and we examine creativity and problem solving in Chapter 5. Based on all the issues covered in Chapters 2 to 5, we then examine in Chapter 6 how we can assess the problem solving process, clearly an important consideration for teachers.

After Chapter 6, we look to broaden our discussions and to examine other activities and processes related to problem solving. Firstly in Chapter 7, we look at other 'open approaches' to mathematics such as investigations and mathematical modelling, and also other approaches to teaching and learning such as the 'realistic mathematics education' approach developed in the Netherlands. In Chapter 8, we examine the issues of enriching children's mathematical experiences and engaging them in the subject, and the role that approaches such as problem solving play in these issues. We conclude in Chapter 9 by reflecting on all the issues that we have discussed in the book, bringing the ideas together in a coherent whole. Throughout each subsequent chapter we ask you some *critical questions* which are designed to make you reflect on your own views of the issues we discuss and to explore your own practice. We also offer you some ideas for *taking it further* by presenting additional reading which we think might help you develop some of the ideas.

In reading this book, we would like you to keep the following quote from Richard Feynman, the Nobel Prize-winning theoretical physicist, in mind:

> *'It doesn't matter how beautiful your theory is, it doesn't matter how smart you are. If it doesn't agree with experiment, it's wrong.'*
>
> Richard Feynman

We know that we have drawn on quite a bit of research in this book to clarify problem solving. We have done this in order to try and get a deeper insight into the issue. But more important than accepting the ideas from the research is how the ideas fit in with your experience, both in terms of doing problem solving and also teaching problem solving. Therefore, we hope you enjoy reflecting upon the ideas in this book and that it does indeed provide you with deeper insights into your experiences of problem solving.

Critical question

»   *At the very outset of this book, what are your own views of problem solving? What do you understand by the term problem solving? What role does it play in your classroom or the classrooms you have observed?*

Taking it further

As identified in the text, Burkart and Bell (2007) provide a historical overview of problem solving in the UK context. In addition, Askew (1996) provides an overview of 'using and applying' in relation to problem solving, but also explores the difficulties that teachers face in coming to understand and teach 'using and applying' in the mathematics classroom.

Askew, M (1996) 'Using and applying mathematics' in schools: reading the texts, in Johnson, D C & Millett, A (eds) *Implementing the Mathematics National Curriculum* (pp. 99–112). London: Paul Chapman Publishing Ltd

Burkart, H, & Bell, A (2007) Problem solving in the United Kingdom. *ZDM*, 39, 395–405

2 What is problem solving?

Key issues in this chapter

- Drawing on the research literature, the chapter begins by considering exactly what is meant by a 'problem' so that you can begin to see what might be involved.

- It then considers the different types of mathematical problems that children tend to experience in the primary classroom.

- Returning to the research, it then focusses on what might be involved in the problem-solving process, which provides the basis for looking at different aspects of this process in subsequent chapters.

- Problem solving is then examined from a classroom perspective, discussing the important issues that you might start to reflect on when considering your practice.

Introduction

As this is a book about problem solving, particularly in the primary mathematics classroom, a sensible starting point is to define precisely what is meant by 'problem solving'. In fact, looking at this term more closely, you can already identify that there are two separate issues to focus upon. Firstly, you need to think about what is meant by the word 'problem'. Secondly, you need to think about what is involved in the 'solving' of these problems; in other words the processes that you go through when you tackle different types of problems. By describing the general processes involved in problem solving, irrespective of the types of problems faced, it is possible to explore the different parts of the problem-solving process in detail (and this is done in subsequent chapters), so that it becomes clear how you can develop children's approaches to tackling mathematical problems. But before we look at these processes, let us define what we mean by a 'problem'.

What is a 'problem'?

Turning to the research literature for a definition of what a problem is, a general definition (not just from mathematics) is given by Kahney (1993): *'Whenever you have a goal which is blocked for any reason – lack of resources, lack of information, so on – you have a problem. Whatever you do in order to achieve your goal is problem solving'* (p.15). Likewise, Mayer (1992) from a psychological perspective identifies three aspects to a problem.

- A problem is in some given state at the start.

- We want it to be in another state (ie we want to solve it).

- There is no obvious way to bring about this change.

Therefore, a simple definition is that a problem is a problem if the route to its solution is not obvious (Jones, 2003). The following is an example of a problem from a Key Stage 2 SATS paper:

> *Liam thinks of a number. He divides it by 9 and then adds 25 to the result. His answer is 36. What number did Liam start with?*

How might you approach this problem? You might think of a variety of ways to solve this. For example, you might work backwards from the answer:

$36 - 25 = 11$

$11 \times 9 = 99$

The answer is 99

Or you might start with an 'unknown':

$(? \div 9) + 25 = 36$

$(? \div 9) = 36 - 25 = 11$

$? = 11 \times 9 = 99$

Or you could use trial and error:

45 ÷ 9 = 5, 5 + 25 = 30 (does not work)

90 ÷ 9 = 10, 10 + 25 = 35 (not quite)

99 ÷ 9 = 11, 11 + 25 = 36 (works!)

Whatever method you choose, and initially you might try a method that does not help you or leads you down a 'blind alley', the way you might approach this problem is not conveyed in the problem itself. There is therefore no specified or obvious approach that you can take to the problem. All you have is the starting 'state' of the problem given above, and you are asked to change this to find the solution.

When is a problem not a problem?

The problem above is an example of a *word problem* and this chapter looks at different types of problems shortly. Orton and Frobisher (1996) give the following word problem as an example of a *routine problem*:

> *How many more than 286 is 637?*

Now, would you regard this as a 'problem' according to the definition given above? Is the route to the solution of this problem obvious or not? Well, you might say that this is dependent on the knowledge and ability of whoever is trying to solve the problem. For a Year 3 child, say, the word *more* may lead them to add the two numbers. Therefore, for them, the route to the solution is not obvious and it is indeed a problem. For a Year 5 child, however, it may be clear to them that subtraction is required and so you can say that this is not a problem for them.

Taking it a step further, would you say that the following is a problem?

$$637 - 286 = ?$$

You might say that this is clearly not a problem as subtraction is obviously required in the question. But how might you do this question? Perhaps a common approach would be to use column subtraction.

$$
\begin{array}{r}
{}^{5}\cancel{6}\,{}^{1}3\;7 \\
2\;8\;6 \\
\hline
3\;5\;1
\end{array}
$$

But you could ask the question 'How else could I do this?' Can you look for other routes to the solution? You might use addition and start from the number to be subtracted:

286 (add 14)   300 (add 300)   600 (add 37)   637

14 + 300 + 37 = 351

And you could try and look for even more routes to the solution, and then decide which approaches you prefer (and this may differ from child to child). What you are doing here is *problematising* the question, which is where children pose or formulate further questions in connection to the original task (Santos-Trigo, 2007). This issue is looked at in more detail in Chapter 4. However, the point here is that even the most routine of questions can be approached from a problem perspective. It depends not only on your existing knowledge, but also on your perspective with regards to how you approach mathematical questions.

Critical questions

»   *From your experience, do you agree or disagree with the definition of a 'problem' as set out above? Why?*

»   *In your practice, or observing other teachers, have you experienced any examples of 'problematising'? If so, how have you or the teacher observed used this approach?*

Types of problems

Having examined exactly what is meant by a 'problem', let us look at the different types of problems, particularly mathematical problems, which are highlighted in the research and also in government literature. Orton and Frobisher (1996) identified three types of mathematical problems: *routine problems*, *environmental problems*, and *process problems*. We gave an example of a routine problem earlier, and Orton and Frobisher define these as problems that *'use knowledge and techniques already acquired by a student in a narrow and synthetic context'* (p. 27). In other words, these are problems closely associated with a particular operation or approach that has most likely already been taught to the children. The emphasis with these problems is on the practise and consolidation of procedures and facts, rather than developing any new understanding.

The second type of problem, environmental problems, are problems set in contexts that are designed to correspond to the real world. Orton and Frobisher (1996) give the example of organising a school competition as an example of an environmental problem. These problems require children to use existing knowledge, both formal mathematical knowledge learnt in the classroom and informal knowledge from the child's broader experience. It is anticipated that bringing together different areas of formal and informal knowledge in the process of tackling such a problem will result in connections being made between these different areas, and thus the children developing their understanding.

The final type of problem given by Orton and Frobisher, the process problems, are problems that focus more particularly on the mathematical thinking processes required to solve the problem, rather than the context of the problem. Unlike the routine problems, they encourage a range of possible approaches to be developed. An example from Orton and Frobisher (1996) is given below:

How many pairs of numbers are there which add up to 475?

We will refer back to these different problem types as we progress through the book.

Turning to government guidance on problems, the DfES (2004) gave the following types of problems that might be used in the primary mathematics classroom:

* word problems (single- and multi-step);
* finding all possibilities;
* logic puzzles;
* finding rules and describing patterns; and
* diagrams/visual puzzles.

Word problems

Word problems alone represent a very diverse range of problems. Apart from the distinct disadvantage of usually being presented via text and so inaccessible to some children, there are at least two other ways in which a word problem can vary; the number of operational steps required to solve it, and whether they are closed- or open-ended. Word problems are often characterised as single- or multi-step and this often refers to the number of operations required to reach the required answer. For instance, an example of a single-step word problem is:

> John has five marbles and Rashid has seven marbles, how many marbles do they have altogether?

On the other hand, the example below is a multi-step word problem because it requires another operational step to solve it:

> John has five marbles and Rashid has seven marbles and they both give two marbles to Shirley. How many marbles do John and Rashid have left?

Closed word problems are those that only require the application of previously acquired knowledge, and we can associate these with the routine problems highlighted earlier. Alternatively, open-ended word problems are those often used in mathematical investigations, where the scope of the problem is unrestricted by the teacher and so determined largely by the ability and imagination of the child or children attempting to solve it. For example, a problem that asks children to *investigate the nature of number patterns in a hundred square* is an open-ended problem. You can see that these relate much more to the process problems highlighted above. Teaching which includes this type of problem can often be fruitful in developing children's motivation, curiosity and enjoyment of mathematics because a large degree of control lies with the child. In this sense, they are inherently differentiating. These types of problems can also be good indicators of children who are mathematically creative because there are no constraints on the number of correct answers. That is, open-ended problems encourage what is referred to as 'divergent' thinking in children, whereas more routine problems encourage 'convergent' thinking where there is only one answer.

Finding all possibilities

An example of a 'finding all possibilities' problem can be seen in Figure 2.1 below. Problems in this category are often aimed at younger children to encourage in them the development of certain generic skills which will be required when attempting all sorts of problems later. For instance, these types of problems aim to develop a systematic approach to problem solving. Consequently, children are often encouraged to start with the smallest number, to check for repeats in their answers, to have a systematic way of recording what they have done and discovered so far (eg in an ordered list or table), and to have a way of knowing when all the possibilities have been found.

Logic puzzles

Logic puzzles require children to use and develop their skills of deductive reasoning (see below). That is, success at such puzzles requires a step-by-step approach to thinking and decision-making where each step and decision follows logically from the previous step. The Sudoku-like puzzle illustrated in Figure 2.2 is a nice example of this. It requires children to complete the 3x3 grid such that each row and each column contains the numbers 1, 2 and 3.

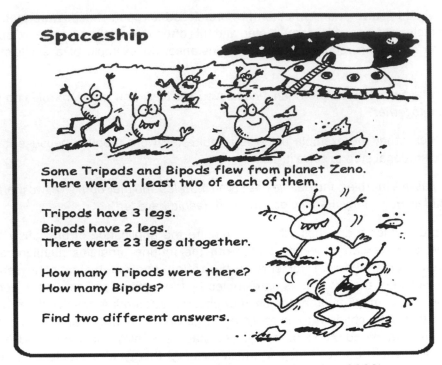

Figure 2.1 *A 'finding all possibilities' problem (DfEE, Crown Copyright 2000)*

Working deductively, children might first decide that the bottom left cell must contain the number 2 (since it cannot contain 1, as there is already 1 in the bottom row and it cannot contain the number 3, because there is already a 3 in the left-hand column and no repeats are allowed). Once this decision is established it will lead logically to other decisions. For instance, it is now logically apparent that the bottom right cell must contain the number 3, because it successfully completes the bottom row.

3		
	1	

Figure 2.2 *A Sudoku-like logic puzzle*

Finding rules and describing patterns

Finding rules and describing patterns are important for encouraging children to work towards developing generalisations in mathematics. This is significant because it involves the children in developing the valuable skills of inductive and deductive reasoning.

Inductive reasoning involves moving from knowledge of specific cases to making predictions about the general case. To use a simple example, children can be encouraged to explore what might happen if they add together any two odd numbers by using specific examples, eg 1 + 3 =?, or 5 + 7 =?, etc. They might quickly become convinced that adding any two odd numbers produces an even number and that this is true for all pairs of odd numbers. The weakness with inductive thinking, however, is that it can never guarantee that this is true for all cases.

Deductive reasoning is much more powerful because it involves generating a general rule and moving from the general statement to a specific case. You can use the language of algebra to generate such a general statement for the case above:

2a + 1 + 2b +1 (where a and b are any integer)

= 2a + 2b + 2

= 2(a + b + 1)

And, reasoning deductively, since a + b + 1 is an integer, then that integer multiplied by 2 must be even.

Diagrams/visual problems

The final type of problems are those that are based on diagrams or which are presented in a visual manner, in contrast to problems that are presented in words or symbols. A simple example taken from Bolt (1982) is given in Figure 2.3, where the question is 'how many triangles are there'?

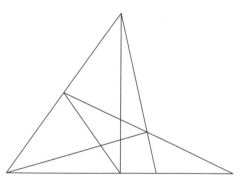

Figure 2.3 *A visual problem*

Here, almost all the information required to tackle the problem is conveyed visually, avoiding the difficulties with language that children can face with word problems as highlighted earlier.

The five types of mathematical problems described above, although by no means comprehensive (and other types of problems will be examined throughout the book), illustrate the range of problems that you can use in the primary classroom, over and above the routine word problems that are often seen.

Critical questions

» Looking at your own practice in schools, or lessons that you have observed, what kind of problems do you commonly see?

» Talk to teachers that you are working with. How do they choose the problems that they give to the children? What considerations do they make?

The problem-solving process

Having described what is meant by a problem and the different types of problems that you might draw upon, let us turn our attention to what is involved in the solving of these problems. Schoenfeld (1992) highlights the importance of the problem-solving 'heuristic' or problem-solving strategy put forward by George Polya (1957) in his influential book *How to solve it*. Polya sets out the following stages to tackling a problem:

- understanding the problem;

- devising a plan;

- carrying out the plan;

- looking back.

In coming to understand the problem, this might involve identifying the unknowns in the problem and also the data you are given. It might also involve changing the format of the problem in order to make sense of it, for example drawing a picture, using different notation, or separating out the different parts of the problem. Devising a plan might mean relating this problem to those that you have done before, or changing the problem to make it more accessible. Having found a route into the problem, the third stage involves carrying out the plan, checking each step of this plan and making sure that it is correct. Having carried out the plan to solve the problem, the final step involves examining the solution again, rechecking the plan, trying to find different ways to obtain the solution, but also considering whether the method used can be transferred to other problems.

Similarities with Polya's model for the problem-solving process can be seen in some of the other processes put forward by researchers. For example, Bransford and Stein (1984, cited in Nickerson, 1994, p. 96) put forward five stages summarised by the acronym IDEAL.

I: Identify the problem.

D: Define and represent the problem.

E: Explore possible strategies.

A: Act on the strategies.

L: Look back and evaluate the effects of your activities.

Alternatively, psychologists view the process as a 'cycle' consisting of the following stages (Pretz, Naples, and Sternberg, 2003, pp. 3–4) as shown in Figure 2.4.

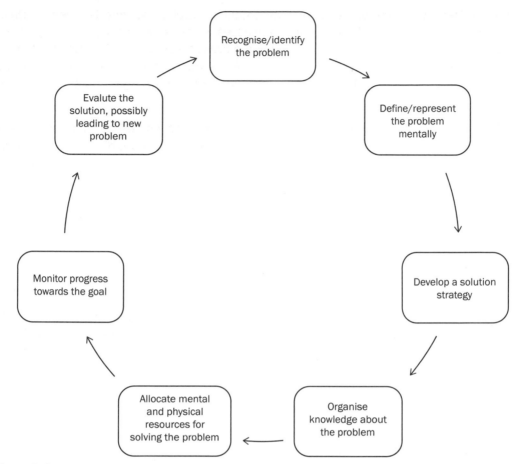

Figure 2.4 *The problem-solving cycle from Pretz, Naples, & Sternberg (2003)*

Looking more specifically at problem-solving approaches in mathematics, Mayer (1992) identified the following steps:

• problem translation;

• problem integration;

• solution planning and monitoring;

• solution execution.

The last two steps are reflected in the processes given above. However a little explanation is required for the first two steps. Problem translation involves representing the problem in a different way (eg translating it from words into a mental image), similar to what is involved in the first of Polya's steps, or step 2 from the cycle given by Pretz, Naples, and Sternberg (2003). Problem integration on the other hand involves connecting the problem, or the translated version of the problem, to existing knowledge or problem 'schemas' (Mayer, 1992, p.466) which can guide the further solving of the problem. Again, this step is echoed in Polya's stage of devising a plan.

A slightly different but related view of mathematical problem solving is given by Davis (1984). He identified two simultaneous processes involved in mathematical problem solving. The first step he referred to as 'building representations' (p.305), reflected in the processes described above, and the second process was referred to as 'meta-analysis' (p.307), or the assessment of progress in tackling the problem, again highlighted in the above processes.

Therefore, in summarising this research on problem-solving processes, it is possible to identify the following key aspects, each of which are explored in more detail in subsequent chapters.

(a)   Identifying the problem – relating the problem to previous experience.

(b)   Representing the problem – interpreting and changing the format of the problem.

(c)   Developing and carrying out a solution strategy.

(d)   Monitoring progress towards the solution.

(e)   Reflecting further on the solution obtained.

These seem to be the important steps in the problem-solving process as reflected by the research. However, you can also look at how the problem-solving process is typically viewed in the primary mathematics classroom, so specific examples from practice are examined in the next section.

Critical questions

»   *Looking at your own practice in schools, or lessons that you have observed, is the problem-solving process made clear to children? If so, how has this process been described to them?*

»   *Choose some mathematical problems to work on (perhaps examples from this chapter). How well do the above processes describe what you do?*

Problem solving in the primary classroom: examples from practice

Monitoring problem solving in schools

Subject leader monitoring (analysis of children's work, SAT papers, lesson observations, etc.) informs the mathematics action plan of the school and will highlight areas for development across the school. More often than not, these areas for development will include problem solving. The first challenge for schools, and also an issue you can explore as you observe practice in schools, is to investigate what it is about problem solving that children find difficult. You can see from our earlier discussion of what problem solving involves that it may be too simplistic to set targets like 'improving problem solving', though this broad statement is often used in school documentation.

Difficulties with problem solving – more than 'the problem'

Deeper analysis of children's understanding should indicate if they have the mathematical skills and prior knowledge to access problems. For example, if children have difficulty calculating they are unlikely to successfully answer the question shown in Figure 2.5, but would you regard this as a problem-solving issue?

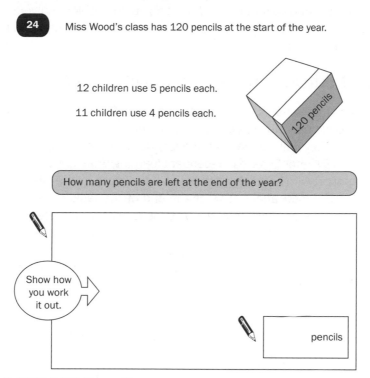

Figure 2.5 *Year 3 2003 SATS Paper 3b*

Similarly, if children have a limited understanding of mathematical vocabulary, eg factors, then the problem in Figure 2.6 may become inaccessible.

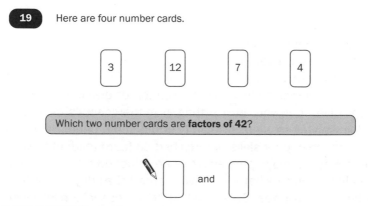

Figure 2.6 *Year 5 2003 SATS Paper A*

This issue may arise if technical vocabulary is not taught, used, heard, discussed and displayed enough in the classroom setting. It could also be that children have limited reading skills, though this should not necessarily hinder their access to problems. Mathematical questions can be read by an adult to a child; or problems can also be acted out before a lesson so children have an understanding of the context; or the vocabulary can be recapped before a lesson to allow children access to the learning. Teachers should be concerned about children's mathematical understanding and their ability to problem solve, not their reading ability, and this might be an issue you consider as you look at difficulties with problem solving in the schools you are working in.

Supporting children with difficulties in problem solving

There are other areas that schools should also consider before identifying problem solving as an issue. How are adults used to support learning in the mathematics classroom? If children receive daily support, they will not become independent thinkers and learners. All children, including those with SEN, should have independent learning time. For example, an adult could give a child initial support with accessing a task and then return a little later to discuss thinking and listen to the child's justifications towards the end of the task. If children always receive support, this will also have an adverse effect on assessment and consequently the planning of appropriate differentiated activities. If work is set at too high a level because the child, with support, is completing the set work, that child will always be reliant on support to access mathematics. It is important to remember that you are teaching problem solving as a life skill and that most children will not always have access to individual support outside of school. Therefore, simply allowing children to work independently on problems may be the issue within a school, rather than an issue specifically with children's problem solving. Look carefully at the kind of support that you observe being given to children when they are problem solving in mathematics.

Incorporating problem solving in the classroom

These and other possible areas of difficulty with regards to problem solving are explored further in the coming chapters. However, mathematics subject leaders and head teachers also need to look at how problem solving is taught throughout the school. Taking into account what is meant by 'problems' and what is involved in problem solving, is it useful to have 'Problem Solving Friday', where children learn a skill during the week, then apply it in a problem-solving context in Friday's lesson? If the children have spent a week practising division, they very soon realise that for the problems set on Friday they will need to divide. This type of activity will support children's application of division, but not necessarily their ability to problem solve. If, in your own setting, it is the school's decision to continue with this weekly problem-solving session, it would be much more beneficial to consider problems requiring a greater range of prior skills, where children learn to identify which skill they need to apply. In other school settings, problems can be attached to the end of the lesson in the plenary. Again, children apply what they have learned that day to solving a problem. This approach is frequently seen in Year 6, where skills are practised and followed by a related SAT-type question to check understanding, but again, does this approach teach children about solving problems or does it consolidate understanding in context? If in your own practice you are asked to take this approach, you may also consider how a broader perspective on problem solving can be provided to the children as well.

In classrooms where independent thinking and learning is valued and where enquiry-based learning is encouraged, teachers may present a problem to the class as an opening activity, facilitating discussion and leading children towards trying out their own strategies to access and ultimately solve the problem. There are many different ways that problem solving and 'using and applying' can be approached in the classroom, some of which are addressed later in this book. Good practice would suggest that a range of approaches should be used depending upon the age and ability of the children. The emphasis should be on the acquisition of pre-requisite skills, including specifically those of problem solving, and also the communicating and reasoning of problem-solving approaches by the children. You might consider whether you have observed, or you yourself use, this kind of approach to problem solving.

It is important that children meet the full range of problem types identified earlier, though in many educational establishments the main focus is still on word problems. When setting problems for the class, you should therefore evaluate your own subject knowledge in relation to the types of problems you are setting. Also, children are very often given a set of rules to follow (such as those represented by the acronyms RUCSAC or QUACK) to access the word problems. RUCSAC stands for:

R: Read

U: Understand (or Underline key facts)

C: Calculate

S: Solve

A: Answer

C: Check

QUACK stands for:

Q: Question – read it carefully

U: Understand – underline

A: Approximate – think about the size of your answer

C: Calculate

K: Know if the answer is sensible or not – check it

This type of acronym is not usually of any support to the more able; they know from prior experience how to access a word problem (and will 'forget' to check whether using the acronym or not!). Nor is it usually of much support to the lower ability children, who may falter at any one of the steps. Neither RUCSAC nor QUACK offer children a route back into a word problem if they become stuck (eg what happens if you 'Read' but then do not 'Understand'?). These acronyms, while offering very little support for word problems, are even less useful for other problem types. Try applying the RUCSAC or QUACK rules to the the example in Figure 2.7 or the visual example given earlier.

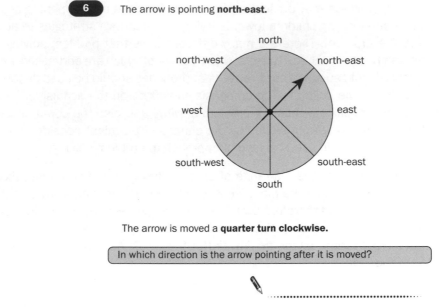

Figure 2.7 *Year 4 2003 SATS Paper B*

Teachers' own lack of understanding of the different types of problems may lead them to think that, by encouraging the use of RUCSAC and QUACK, they are providing a support for problem solving. However, as previously stated, these are of little or no benefit to the majority of children in learning how to problem solve. The research examined earlier indicates that the problem-solving process is more complex than these simple acronyms suggest and children need to learn the different skills of accessing and solving all problem types. The suitability of these acronyms to support access to word problems or any other type of problem is discussed in more detail in later chapters. For now, you can consider whether this is the approach that you see or use yourself when incorporating problem solving into your teaching.

Broader links to using and applying

It is also necessary that schools investigate how the other aspects of using and applying are taught throughout the school. Observations have shown that children can apply skills to a problem with very little understanding of how to problem solve. It is therefore crucial if you are to inculcate a positive attitude to problem solving and an environment where children continue to search for solutions beyond the first hurdle, that you combine it with teaching children the skills of communicating their understanding and reasoning about mathematics. These two areas of using and applying are often less apparent in primary teaching, perhaps because of teachers' attitudes towards and confidence in the subject. Schools, and you yourself, should consider the following questions:

- Are the skills of communicating and reasoning taught or assumed?

- Do we follow progressive guidelines that build on prior understanding?

- Does our teaching facilitate independent learning, 'searching for a solution by trying out ideas of their own' (MA1 Using and Applying, reasoning, Level 4)?

- Does our classroom ethos encourage children to decide themselves how best to represent conclusions (MA1 Using and Applying, communicating, Level 5) and to form their own generalisations (MA1 Using and Applying, reasoning, Level 4)?

When you enter a new school as a trainee or teacher it is important to find answers to these questions to inform your teaching.

There is much to consider when a school concludes that they need to, or would like to, focus on improving problem-solving skills. As an educator it is your role to ensure that these considerations go beyond finding out what a child cannot do and that you take a broader look at how you approach problem solving.

Critical questions

» In schools that you work with, what are the difficulties that children have with problem solving? What reasons are given for these difficulties and how do they relate to the research we have discussed on problems and problem solving?

» How are children who have difficulties with problem solving supported in the classroom?

» How is problem solving incorporated into the classrooms that you have experienced? What are the strengths and /or weaknesses in the approaches that you have observed?

Critical reflections

In summarising this chapter, if there is one key message, it is the importance of considering in detail the problem-solving process involved. As the early considerations from the research of what a problem actually is demonstrated, simply considering this question raises some interesting issues with regards to how problem solving in the primary classroom can be approached. Should you set aside time to do 'problems', perhaps at the end of the school week as highlighted in the examples from practice, or could you adopt a broader problem-solving perspective in the classroom, by encouraging children to 'problematise' the mathematics that they are doing? This broader perspective is also reflected in the different types of mathematical problems that you can draw upon in your teaching – once again, this is not just the focus on word problems that is often seen in the classroom context.

This detailed consideration of problem solving is even more important when the processes involved in problem solving are considered. You have seen examples from the classroom of ways in which teachers try to guide children in their approach to tackling problems. However, you have also seen that approaches such as RUCSAC and QUACK may remain unhelpful if it is not made clear to children exactly what is involved in these procedures.

These detailed considerations begin to uncover the areas of difficulty that children face in problem solving – for example, when looking to improve the teaching of problem solving in the classroom context, there are issues such as language, calculation knowledge, or even the lack of experience of working independently, that might impact on children's abilities to problem solve. The detailed considerations made throughout the rest of this book provide more specific support for teachers in tackling these difficulties. The first step that you need to take is to be willing to look at the problem-solving process and to make these considerations.

Taking it further

Perhaps the classic text on problem solving, and one that we have referred to in this chapter, is George Polya's *How to solve it*. Not only does this text try and break down the problem-solving process at the start of the book, but the section entitled *'In the classroom'* gives examples of what this process looks like (although admittedly not particularly from a primary perspective).

Another classic text is *Thinking mathematically* by John Mason, Leone Burton and Kaye Stacey. They provide another view of the problem-solving process, based on the phases of 'Entry', 'Attack' and 'Review' with lots of examples of problems relevant to the primary classroom. There are also some nice suggestions concerning what to do when you are stuck on a problem.

Polya, G (1957) *How to solve it: A new aspect of mathematical method*. New York: Doubleday Anchor Books

Mason, J, Burton, L, & Stacey, K (1985) *Thinking mathematically*. Wokingham: Addison-Wesley Publishing Company

3 Representing problems

Key issues in this chapter

- The chapter begins by exploring how we come to 'understand' problems and the importance therein of representing or reformulating problems.

- In doing so, it defines exactly what we mean by a 'representation', including what we term as *internal* and *external* representations.

- Having defined representations, it clarifies the process of using representations in problem solving, and, additionally, highlighting the importance of prior knowledge in this process.

- It also explores the notion of language as a representation, and highlights the importance of discussion as a way of making sense of this and other representations of problems.

Introduction

The last chapter summarised the processes involved in problem solving. These included:

(a) identifying the problem – relating the problem to previous experience;

(b) representing the problem – interpreting and changing the format of the problem.

This chapter looks in more detail at the process of representing the problem. In doing this we will take a slight detour and look more broadly at what is meant by 'representing' and 'representations'. In doing so, we connect with ideas such as what we mean by 'understanding' a problem, the importance of prior knowledge in problem solving (relating to the first of the processes given above), and the role that language plays in problem solving. Although these may seem to be a diverse range of ideas to include in the same chapter, we hope to show that they are all underpinned by the view of representations that we put forward.

Understanding the problem

Returning for a moment to the ideas covered in the previous chapter, we draw again upon Polya's influential view of the problem-solving heuristic (Polya, 1957). The first step in his process involves 'understanding the problem'. Looking in more detail at what Polya says, he highlights two possibly related actions of 'getting acquainted' with the problem and 'working for better understanding'. Doing the first of these, Polya suggests that you begin with the problem and try to visualise the problem as a whole.

> You should understand the problem, familiarize yourself with it, impress its purpose on your mind. The attention bestowed on the problem may also stimulate your memory and prepare for the recollection of relevant points.
>
> (Polya, 1957, p.33)

The importance of prior relevant knowledge emerges already in this first step. Polya also goes on to suggest that we work for better understanding by looking at the different parts of the problem, and relating the different parts to each other or to the whole. Polya states that this 'decomposing and recomposing' (p.75) of a problem allows the problem to become more accessible to the solver. In fact we would say that this is already beginning to show the importance of 'representing' the problem, ie changing the problem into another format.

Gestalt view of problem solving

This idea of 'representing' is highlighted by Mayer (1992) as being the way Gestalt psychologists conceptualised the idea of problem solving. This Gestalt view of psychology was developed in Germany at the start of the twentieth century, prior to the Second World War. Mayer highlights that the key idea in this school of psychology is that people make sense of external stimuli through the imposing of order and structure on the stimuli concerned. For example, the Gestalt view of problem solving involves people trying to understand how the elements of a problem fit together and reorganising the elements into a new structure to further aid understanding. This is similar to Polya's decomposing and recomposing. Mayer also highlights the two kinds of thinking identified by the Gestalt approach. We have reproductive thinking, where established ways of thinking are reproduced. We also have productive thinking, where through the reorganising of the information, new ways of thinking are achieved. This productive thinking is very often associated with creative thinking, with accompanied flashes of insight, and we will look in more detail into this creative problem-solving process in Chapter 5.

It is helpful here to give a concrete example of the process described above, and we draw on the example of 'reformulation' provided by Watts (1991) in his book on problem solving for science teachers. He highlighted that representing or reformulation can be done in a number of ways. We will give different examples later of the types of representations that we can draw upon in carrying out this reformulation. More simply though, one can talk through the problem with someone else (we will also refer to this later when looking at language) – this simple act of reorganising the problem for the purposes of discussion is a form of representing. Alternatively, we can try trial and error, which in turn is reformulating the problem with different possible solutions to see what happens. In time this may become more systematic. Watts gives the example of a person fixing a car, *'fiddling with leads, connections, prodding, poking, knocking, etc.'* (p.32). This may start speculatively but, in fact, reformulates the car problem by isolating the problem to a more localised area of the engine. We see that the representing of problems may include quite mundane processes which provide insight into a problem.

Critical questions

» *How does this view of representing match your approach to problem solving; for example when you tackle a word problem? In what ways do you represent the problem or do you try and solve it straight away?*

» *How do children that you work with represent their problems? Is this only through underlining or highlighting key parts of a problem, or do they use other approaches such as drawings or using concrete materials?*

» *What other ways can you think of for representing a problem?*

The idea of representations

We have begun to explore the notion of understanding problems and the role that reorganising the problems plays in this understanding process. Let us look a little more carefully at what we mean by representations. In general, Kaput (1985) defines a representation as *'something that stands for something else'* (p.383). More specifically, we make the distinction between *internal* and *external* manifestations of representations (Pape and Tchoshanov, 2001), or 'mental structures' and 'notation systems' as referred to by Kaput (1991). Davis (1984) describes internal representations in mathematics as *'any mathematical concept, or technique, or strategy ... if it is to be present in my mind at all, must be* represented *in some way'* (p.203). Likewise, Kaput (1985) highlights that cognitive psychologists are in agreement that sentient organisms represent mentally or internally their experience of the environment. Therefore, although we cannot access our internal representations of concepts directly (which is why it is so hard to pin down what they are), we can agree that we do internally represent mathematical stimuli in our minds. Alternatively, external representations or notation systems are easier to identify. External representations are *'materially instantiated'* entities (Kaput 1991, p.56), such as physical apparatus, marks on paper, pictures, symbols, sounds and spoken/written words.

How do representations help?

We highlighted previously the important notion of reformulating or representing the original problem in a different way. Let us say more about the role that representations play in problem solving. Mayer (1992) highlights another way in which representations aid understanding of problems. Representations, or more particularly external representations, help by making abstract ideas more concrete (and this point is also highlighted by amongst others Duval, 1999, and Flevares and Perry, 2001). Let us look at an example. A difficult problem for young children is a comparison problem involving subtraction. For example, 'Lynn has 5 sweets, and David has 8 sweets. How many more sweets does David have than Lynn?' One of the difficult aspects of this word problem is that the word 'more' can mislead children to thinking this requires an addition operation. However, we could ask children to represent this in a concrete way (we will represent the problem with a drawing as shown in Figure 3.1).

Lynn

David

Figure 3.1 *Representing a comparison problem in a more concrete way.*

Representing the problem in a more concrete way will hopefully allow children to interpret and understand what the problem is asking for. Although Mayer emphasises the 'concrete' nature of representations, as our example above has shown, diagrams and drawings can aid problem solving as well. Other studies have highlighted this beneficial impact. For example, Pantziara, Gagatsis and Elia (2009) carried out a study with 194 grade 6 Cypriot children (final year of primary school), where the children were given problems with and without accompanying diagrams. By diagrams, we mean more abstract drawings with minimal details presented within the figure. This is as opposed to drawings, which would contain more unnecessary details, the above being such an example. The researchers found that children performed significantly better on problems with diagrams compared to those without. In another study, encouraging young children (age 9) in Hungary to draw representations for themselves for word and arithmetic problems also had a significant impact (Csíkos, Szitányi, and Kelemen, 2012).

The process of representing problems

In making clear the idea of 'representations', we have reiterated the points made earlier by Polya and Mayer amongst others regarding the importance of representing problems during the solving process. We can go still further with this. Kahney (1993) suggests that how we mentally or internally represent a problem is one of the most important determinants of whether we can solve a problem. The way we internally represent such problems will in turn relate to the ways in which we can externally represent or reformulate problems. The studies from Pantziara et al (2009) and Csíkos et al (2012) provide possible evidence for this link between external representations and the process of representing problems.

Examples – isomorphic problems

Let us look at another example to emphasise this importance. This is quite a convoluted problem so bear with us! We have a King, a Prince and a Duke on a camping trip. Each day, while camping, there are three jobs to do between them, although one of them could do more than one job. The jobs are:

*   collect firewood (first task);

*   light the fire (second task);

*   cook the meals (third task).

They have to make sure the jobs are done in order, otherwise they will be trying to light a non-existent fire or not being able to cook. On the first day, the King did all the jobs. However, in the days that followed, he decided to transfer the jobs between the others, with the condition that he could only transfer one job between any of the three of them each day, and making sure that if a person then had more than one job to do, they were in the right order. Also, when transferring a job from a person, only their first job could be transferred (if they had more than one to do). Eventually, he wanted all the jobs to be done by the Duke (the least important). What is the least number of days it would take the King to transfer the jobs? Before you read on, try and solve this problem yourself.

OK, how did you do? Did you find that easy or hard? Was it hard to decipher the question? (We found it hard!) What strategies did you use? From what we have talked about so far in this chapter, you might have tried to reformulate this problem. How did you do that? We suggest that whether you found this problem easy or hard to do would depend on how you internally represented this problem (involving the deciphering), which in turn would have been helped by any external representations that you could draw upon. So, did you use jottings to make sense of the problems? Did you draw a picture? In fact, we may help you by giving you a problem that has the same 'structure', and is referred to as an *isomorphic* problem.

The Tower of Hanoi problem is a famous example given in problem solving literature. The problem is as follows.

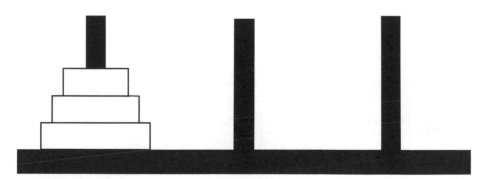

Figure 3.2 *The Tower of Hanoi problem*

The problem involves three rings (small, medium, large) on one of three 'pegs', arranged with the largest at the bottom and the smallest at the top. In the problem, we can move one ring at a time on to another peg, with the one proviso that you cannot move a larger ring on top on a smaller ring. The aim of the problem is to find a way of moving all the rings from one peg to another. Again, have a go at solving this problem before reading on.

So, how did you do the Tower of Hanoi problem? Did you actually get some concrete objects (say different sized coins and maybe three circles on a piece of paper) and try the problem that way? Or did you represent it a different way? Given below is one approach the authors tried.

This solution method involved organising the different possible combinations for the problem in a table. Now, if we ask you to go back and tackle the camping problem, how would you do it this time (have a go)? It may be that your solution method this time would look something like this:

Table 3.1 *One possible solution to the Tower of Hanoi problem*

Move	Peg 1	Peg 2	Peg 3
0	S,M,L		
1	M,L	S	
2	L	S	M
3	L		S,M
4		L	S,M
5	S	L	M
6	S	M,L	
7		S,M,L	

Table 3.2 *One possible solution to the camping problem*

Day	King	Prince	Duke
0	Wood, Fire, Meal		
1	Fire, Meal		Wood
2	Meal	Fire	Wood
3	Meal	Wood, Fire	
4		Wood, Fire	Meal
5	Wood	Fire	Meal
6	Wood		Fire, Meal
7			Wood, Fire, Meal

You may need a couple of goes to make sure that the jobs end up with the right person. However, hopefully you can see that otherwise, the structure of the two problems is identical, therefore having a way (a representation) for solving one feeds into the solution for the other.

The solving of the Tower of Hanoi problem has provided us with an internal representation for solving the camping problem. Note that this is not just about having a 'picture' in one's mind; the internal representation might be a more complete process (which might include pictures) which helps us to solve additional, similar problems.

The role of prior knowledge

What the above example also illustrates is the importance of the prior knowledge that the problem solver brings to any given problem. In the example, once we had experience of the Tower of Hanoi problem, then we could see the camping problem in a different way. (Or we might say that we might internally represent the camping problem in a different way). As a result, our previous experience helped us to solve the particular problem.

The benefits of prior knowledge

This important role that prior knowledge and experience play in the problem-solving process is widely recognised by researchers. For example, Pretz et al (2003) highlight the difference between 'experts' and 'novices' in terms of their experience of solving problems in a particular topic area. Expert problem solvers often *'have more efficient representations of their domain than do novices. These representations have stripped away irrelevant details and get at the deeper structure of the problem'* (p.13). This links back to the previous research by Pantziara et al (2009) encouraging children to use diagrams. The fact that prior knowledge and experience is an important part of successful problem solving shows the important role that prior instruction and teaching can play in the process.

We can take this view of prior knowledge a step further, by considering how this knowledge impacts on the way that a solver perceives a problem. We can observe this through an example. Figure 3.3 shows a cube (known as the Necker cube by psychologists).

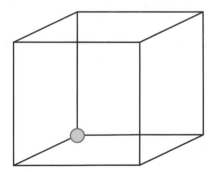

Figure 3.3 *The Necker cube*

The Necker cube simply shows a two-dimensional picture of a three-dimensional cube. In the picture, we included a grey spot to show the position of one of the corners of the cube. Now, the question is where exactly is the spot relative to the cube? Take a few moments to look at the cube. Unless you have come across this example before, regardless of how long you look at the cube, you will say that the position of the spot is definitely in a given position relative to the cube. This position is going to be either the back, bottom, left-hand corner of the cube, or the front, bottom, left-hand corner. But wait a minute! How can the spot be in two different possible positions? It is all about how you perceive the example. Take a look at the cube again. If you only saw it in one position last time, try and see the cube from the other perspective. So, if the spot was at the back last time, try and see the cube with the spot at the front, or vice versa. It may take some moments before you see this, but then you may experience the strange occurrence of the cube 'flipping' as you look at it; the front flipping to the back or the reverse. The more you look at it, the more you may consciously alter your perspective. Can you see what has happened now? Having the different perspective pointed out to you, and therefore developing your knowledge, has allowed you to perceive the example in a different way. As put succinctly by Gregory (2009, p.52), *'Eyes provide sensory signals but knowledge is needed to convert seeing into perceiving'*. In other words, how we perceive and make sense of a problem is dependent on our existing knowledge, as we saw from the Tower of Hanoi and camping examples. If we were to give you another example now, you would probably try and work out whether the problem was isomorphic to the Tower of Hanoi example. Through developing your knowledge, this time through instruction, we develop the ways in which you internally represent the problem and therefore facilitate the problem-solving process.

The drawbacks of prior knowledge

Going back to the types of problems highlighted in the previous chapter, what we very often see are teachers practising particular types of problems with children, whether they are single- or multi-step word problems, logic problems or whatever. We see from the above that this practice impacts on the prior knowledge of children, and supports the process of appropriately representing problems that they face. Mayer (1992) further emphasises the positive effects of past experiences on the problem-solving process. Interestingly, however, Mayer also highlights the negative aspects of past experiences as well. The particular negative aspects that he highlights are rigidity in the problem-solving process or what he terms *'functional fixedness'*. This rigidity or fixedness is described as when *'the reproductive application of past habits inhibits productive problem solving'* (Mayer, 1992, p.54). An example given by Mayer, from Duncker (1945), is the following problem. You are given three candles, three drawing pins and three matches, each group of items in a cardboard box. The goal of the problem is to mount a candle on a nearby screen to act as a lamp. Looking at the arrangement in Figure 3.4, think for a minute or so about how you would go about the problem.

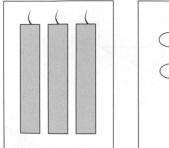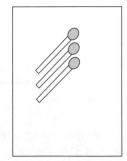

Figure 3.4 Duncker's problem

Did you come up with a solution? Let us present the problem in a slightly different way, with the objects outside of the boxes as in Figure 3.5.

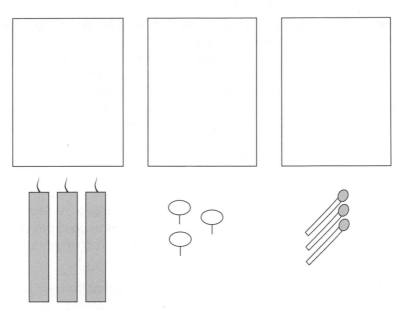

Figure 3.5 *Duncker's problem modified*

Now think about the problem again. The hoped-for solution was actually to use one of the boxes as part of the solution (as Figure 3.6 illustrates).

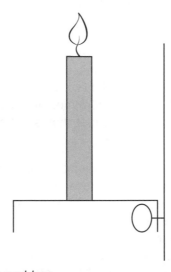

Figure 3.6 *Solution to Duncker's problem*

Were you able to think creatively and use one of the boxes in the first presentation of the problem as part of the solution? Or did you find it easier when, in the second presentation, the boxes were actually presented separately to their contents? Mayer highlights that studies which have looked at Duncker's problem find that people are twice as likely to reach a solution when presented with the problem in the second format, compared to those presented with the first format. This is explained by the fact that in the first format, the boxes are 'pre-utilised' and fixed in their function, making it more difficult for people to reformulate their use. This does not occur in the second formulation. What this example highlights is that we can become fixed in our approaches to problems, as we may have been fixed on the use of the boxes, owing to our previous knowledge and experiences. Therefore, we must be aware that being fixed or rigid in our approach to solving problems can have a negative impact. At times, we must question the approaches we are taking, perhaps try different representations or procedures in solving a problem, to develop our ability to solve a problem. We look at this process of questioning or 'problematising' in the next chapter.

Critical questions

» *From your experience, what is the role, in problem solving, of remembering prior methods when tackling a particular type of problem? How does this approach compare to other, previously highlighted approaches to representing? Do children seem more comfortable with one or the other or both?*

» *What kind of pitfalls exist for children when they are trying to recall previous approaches to a type of problem?*

» *An approach to problem solving that we have not considered here is that of estimating the answer. How does estimation fit in with the issues of representing that we have discussed so far?*

Language as a representation

Another aspect of representation that we consider in the problem-solving process is the role played by language, particularly in the case of word problems. In the camping problem given above, the problem was initially given in a representation using written language. The initial challenge of that problem was to decipher what the words were saying, and then to re-present the problem in a format that was more meaningful to the solver. In this section, we consider language as a representational format that is often used with problems, and what that means for the problem-solving process.

Firstly, it is important to recognise that language is just that – a representation. Brune (1953) highlighted the following with regards to language. We must remember that words are 'chains' in the communication process between people, and that words (obviously including mathematical words) often represent mental constructs rather than actual tangible concepts. In relation to this, we must remember that the words being used in any communication are symbols, standing for some construct, and the words we use for constructs develop through agreements between people, rather than containing some absolute meaning within. An example will explain these ideas more clearly (recognising the deficiencies in the way we represent the ideas through words!).

In Figure 3.7, one person is trying to convey the concept of a small, furry mouse to the other. But the other person can interpret that representation of the spoken word in their own way (in the example, as a computer mouse). We can see that the way we use and interpret words can be different for different people; they are personal representations for each person. There are of course countless examples of such personal interpretations of words causing

Figure 3.7 *Language as representations*

confusion. The famous painting by the surrealist painter René Magritte entitled 'The Treachery of Images' shows a picture of a pipe (as in one you would smoke), with the words *'Ceci n'est pas une pipe'* (This is not a pipe) written beneath the pipe. Magritte explained that as he could not fill this pipe with tobacco, then of course it was not a pipe – just a representation of one! In mathematical contexts too, we see the 'treachery' of language. Wood (1998, p. 262) gives the following example.

Interviewer: *Do you know what volume means?*

Child: *Yes.*

Interviewer: *Could you explain to me what it means?*

Child: *Yes, it's what is on the knob of the television set.*

Therefore, going back to Polya's first step in his heuristic of *'understanding the problem'*, in the case of problems represented by written or spoken language, this first step involved understanding the intended meaning from the problems.

Specialised use of language in mathematics

Staying on this issue of difficulties with language, mathematics as a subject is vulnerable to this because of the specialised use of words in some mathematical contexts. For example, Nicholson (1977) carried out a study with secondary school children, where they were asked to solve different problems involving mathematical terms. Examples of these were: *'What is the product of 15 and 3?'*; *'Give an example of a multiple of 30'*. Nicholson examined whether they solved the problems correctly, left the answer blank, or were confused in their answer.

Table 3.3 Difficulties with mathematical language (from Nicholson, 1977, pp. 32–33)

Word	Correct	Blank	Confused
Multiply	99.5	0	0.5
Remainder	98	0	2
Factor	91	5	4
Reflection	86.5	0.5	13
Parallel	86	5	9
Square root	81.5	3	15
Intersection	75.5	3	21
Square number	75	4	21
Prime number	68.5	9.5	21.5
Parallelogram	65.5	5.5	29
Rectangle	64.5	4.5	31.5
Union	55	5	40
Mapping	41	32.5	26.5
Rotation	34.5	6	59.5
Rhombus	32.5	24	44
Product	20.5	4.5	75
Multiple	11.5	2	86.5
Integer	9.5	18.5	72

Looking at the above list, although this is a relatively old piece of research, you may be surprised by some of the words that caused difficulty. For example, integer, multiple, rhombus, and rotation; these are all mathematical words which we would expect children to be comfortable with at the end of primary school. The word 'product' is an interesting one in that, like the example of 'volume' given earlier, these words have both a mathematical meaning, and also a different 'real world' meaning.

Children with English as an additional language

In considering the issues around language being a representation that we have to interpret, it is relevant to link to research that highlights the difficulties that children with English as an Additional Language (EAL) have. This is important because very often, difficulties with working in English may be mistaken for difficulties with the actual mathematics (Ellerton and Clarkson, 1996). There have been a number of international studies looking specifically at the difficulties EAL children may have with problems, particularly word problems. Clarkson (1991) carried out a study in Papua New Guinea (PNG) looking at what specific difficulties children working in the additional language of English had with tackling word problems. Clarkson divided up the problem-solving process into the following processes: reading the problem; comprehending the problem; transforming the problem into a format for calculation (or representing); processing or calculating the problem; and, finally, encoding or finalising the answer to the problem. You can see that this is another variation on the problem-solving process, related more to word problems, but still bearing strong similarities to the processes highlighted in the last chapter. In identifying these different stages, Clarkson was then able to see where different children had difficulties. He found that PNG Year 6 children made more mistakes in the area of reading and, particularly, comprehension compared to Australian Year 6 children. However, in other stages of the problem-solving process, the proportion of children making mistakes in these areas was broadly the same. This study highlights the particular difficulty for EAL children in gaining the appropriate meaning from written English, ie the difficulty of interpreting the written representation of the problem.

In a related study by Bautista, Mitchelmore and Mulligan (2009) with Filipino children, they explored whether it would help if they additionally read aloud the problem in English or presented the written problem in Filipino. They found that reading aloud in English had no significant benefit for the children compared to presenting the problems in written English. On the other hand, presenting the problems in Filipino did have a significant impact. Once again, this study demonstrated that it is the comprehension of the problem in a different language, rather than the reading process per se, that leads to difficulties for EAL children. It is the representation of the problem in a format that they do not understand, as in the examples for non-EAL children given above, which leads to problems for EAL children.

Supporting children with language

Thinking of language as a representation then, how can we as teachers deal with the problematic nature of language? Does the fact that children interpret language in their own way simply lead to chaos in the classroom? In fact, we can try and tackle this issue of language on two levels. Firstly, as a teacher, we can directly monitor and support children in their interpretations of language. Durkin and Shire (1991) make a number of suggestions with respect to this. Firstly, in communication with children (either in spoken or written language), we can try to be aware of 'lexical ambiguity' in the words that we are using. Can we try and spot beforehand potential problems that some children may have? (For example, the meanings of 'volume' and 'product' highlighted above.) In recognising these potential problems, we can actually take advantage of them and use them as learning opportunities for children by actively introducing them to new uses of particular words. Also, and going back to our earlier discussion on representations and problem solving, we can provide further visual or concrete support for children to make sense of the language. For example, might a helpful picture or diagram support the child in interpreting the problem? This is slightly different to providing a representation which supports the calculation process, as we saw in the example of the compare subtraction problem given earlier. The use of additional representations in this case is to specifically support the interpretation of the language. Skemp (1989) also provides some suggestions for supporting children. He suggests that teachers stay with spoken language when teaching mathematics, especially in the earlier years of primary school, because for these younger children their connection to spoken language is stronger than with written language. Also, in moving to written language, allow for 'transitional' language, rather than the formal language used, to support children in moving towards the formal mathematical terms.

The role of discussion

The above suggestions try to tackle more directly the issues of language. However, we can support children in a different way. Rather than directly dealing with problems, we can support children in order to try and make sense of the language involved. For example, simply discussing the issue may help children to make sense of problems, drawing upon knowledge that they may not initially realise that they possess (Wood, 1998). Hoyles et al (1991) look in more detail at the role that discussion can play in the mathematics classroom. They distinguish different aspects of discussion, including the following.

- Discussion provides 'distancing' – articulating your thoughts allows you to stand back and examine the way you have represented the idea (in this case your interpretation of the problem) and, if necessary, to modify this representation.

- Discussion provides conflict – to bring together different representations or perspectives from different people possibly leading to re-evaluation in these perspectives.

- Discussion supports scaffolding – the discussion process allows others to support the individual in their construction of ideas (or interpretation of problems in this case).

Although these are general aspects of discussion (not necessarily confined to mathematics), we can see how discussion can benefit the child in interpreting the language involved in a problem. The child can therefore hopefully construct an appropriate internal representation of the problem, which in turn supports them in solving the problem.

Critical questions

» *From your experience, what are typical examples of difficulties with language within problem solving that you come across? Are there particular mathematical terms or areas of mathematics that cause frequent language difficulties for children?*

» *What ways do you use to support children with language and problem solving?*

Furthermore, if you have experience of working with children whose first language is not English, what additional ways do you use to support these children in mathematics?

Representing the problem – the classroom perspective

From a practical classroom perspective, representing problems is at the heart of the new national curriculum (DfE, 2013). It aims to ensure that children *'can solve problems by applying their mathematics to a variety of routine and non-routine problems with increasing sophistication, including breaking down problems into a series of simpler steps and persevering in seeking solutions'* (DfE, 2013, p.3). In the new curriculum, Programmes of Study are organised into the distinct domains of number, measurement, geometry and statistics. In a change from the previous curriculum, using and applying is no longer a separate area, but instead is integral to all topics. See below how these topics are covered across year groups (Table 3.4) and how problem solving is identified within the areas (Table 3.5).

Table 3.5 sets out the problem-solving expectations of the new national curriculum and you can see that it is expected that children begin to represent problems from as early as Year 1: *'Solve one-step problems that involve addition and subtraction using concrete objects and pictorial representations...'*. In schools, teachers should help children to see that representing is part of the problem-solving process and children should be encouraged to use and develop the skill of representing as they progress through school. Unfortunately, in some schools, representing a problem in this way is seen as a stage that the children are at and which they will 'grow out of' once they learn the rules and become more proficient problem solvers. Being neat (which is NOT the same as being systematic) tends to become more of a focus as children move through year groups. While it is helpful to be organised in order to minimise mistakes, check working and reflect upon strategies and routes (which we will highlight in the next chapter), this focus can hinder children's desire to represent on paper. Many schools cite Ofsted and school book scrutinies as the reason for this development. However, as educators, we must have an understanding of how children learn to solve problems and be able to argue that the neatest books do not always show the best learning. It is common in Year 6 to hear teachers encourage children to represent problems on their SAT papers – draw a picture, annotate a diagram, etc. They are 'unteaching' what has gone before, that pages must be clean and neat, but they do this because they know that, by representing the problem in some way, the children are more likely to arrive at a satisfactory conclusion.

As stated already, representing is a skill that should be developed as children progress through school, and therefore time should be given in lessons for children to practise this. The teacher could present a problem at the beginning of a lesson then split children into groups to work on representing it in different ways. A mini-plenary could be used to share ideas, which could include acting out the problem, drawing diagrams and tables, setting it in a different context or using different numbers, etc., before children begin to look for a solution. The main plenary could be used to discuss the efficacy of different representations and to reflect on learning.

Table 3.4 *National Curriculum 2013 – topics covered by year group*

		Y1	Y2	Y3	Y4	Y5	Y6
Number	number and place value	✓	✓	✓	✓	✓	✓
	addition and subtraction	✓	✓	✓	✓	✓	✓
	multiplication and division	✓	✓	✓	✓	✓	
	fractions	✓	✓	✓			
	fractions and decimals				✓		
	fractions, decimals and percentages					✓	✓
	ratio and proportion						✓
	algebra						✓
Measurement		✓	✓	✓	✓	✓	✓
Geometry	properties of shapes	✓	✓	✓	✓	✓	✓
	position and direction	✓	✓		✓	✓	✓
Statistics			✓	✓	✓	✓	✓

In relation to the consideration of language as a representation that we use for problems, children may throughout this process need support to understand mathematical terminology, and it is useful to consider what strategies can be used in the classroom to aid understanding. The questions that we might ask are:

- do the children have access to mathematical dictionaries?
- are children introduced to new words and their meanings at the beginning of a topic and are these reviewed at the end of a topic?
- is there a vocabulary board/working wall that is used effectively by the children?

Mathematical dictionaries are available in book form and online (including dictionaries in dual languages) and should be as readily available as rulers and pencils in the classroom. Once children have identified the meaning of a word for themselves, they could add it to the

Table 3.5 *The demands of the new national curriculum 2013, problem solving – statutory requirements*

		Y1	Y2	Y3	Y4	Y5	Y6
Number	number and place value		Use place value and number facts to solve problems	Solve number problems and practical problems	Solve number and practical problems with increasingly large positive numbers	Solve number problems and practical problems	Solve number and practical problems
	addition and subtraction	Solve one-step problems that involve addition and subtraction, using concrete objects and pictorial representations, and missing number problems.	Solve problems with addition and subtraction: *Using concrete objects and pictorial representations, including those involving numbers, quantities and numbers *applying their increasing knowledge of mental and written methods.	Solve problems, including missing number problems, using number facts, place value, and more complex addition and subtraction.	Solve addition and subtraction two-step problems in contexts, deciding which operations and methods to use and why.	Addition and subtraction multi-step problems in contexts, deciding which operations and methods to use and why.	

Table 3.5 (cont.)

	Y1	Y2	Y3	Y4	Y5	Y6
multiplication and division	Solve one-step problems involving multiplication and division, by calculating the answer using concrete objects, pictorial representations and arrays with support from the teacher.	Solve problems involving multiplication and division, using materials, arrays, repeated addition, mental methods and multiplication and division facts, including problems in contexts.	Solve problems, including missing number problems, involving multiplication and division, including positive integer scaling problems and correspondence problems in which n objects are connected to m objects.	Solve problems involving multiplying and adding, including using the distributive law to multiply two digit numbers by one digit, integer scaling problems and harder correspondence problems such as n objects are connected to m objects.	Solve problems involving multiplication and division including using their knowledge of factors and multiples, squares and cubes. Solve problems involving addition, subtraction, multiplication and division and combinations of these, including understanding the meaning of the equals sign. Solve problems involving multiplication and division, including scaling by simple fractions and problems involving simple rates.	Solve addition and subtraction multi-step problems in contexts, deciding which operations and methods to use and why. Solve problems involving addition, subtraction, multiplication and division.
fractions			Solve problems.			

					Solve problems which require answers to be rounded to specified degrees of accuracy.
fractions and decimals	Solve problems involving increasingly harder fractions to calculate quantities, and fractions to divide quantities, including non-unit fractions where the answer is a whole number. Solve simple measure and money problems involving fractions and decimals to two decimal places.				
fractions, decimals and percentages				Solve problems involving numbers up to three decimal places which require knowing percentage and decimal equivalent of 1/2, 1/4, 1/5, 2/5 and 4/5 and those fractions with a denominator of a multiple of 10 or 25.	

Table 3.5 (cont.)

	Y1	Y2	Y3	Y4	Y5	Y6
ratio and proportion						Solve problems involving the relative sizes of two quantities where missing values can be found by using integer multiplication and division facts. Solve problems involving the calculation of percentages and the use of percentages for comparison. Solve problems involving similar shapes where the scale factor is known or can be found. Solve problems involving unequal sharing and grouping using knowledge of fractions and multiples.

algebra	Compare, describe and solve practical problems.				
Measurement	Solve simple problems in a practical context involving addition and subtraction of money of the same unit, including giving change.		Solve problems involving converting from hours to minutes; minutes to seconds; years to months; weeks to days.	Solve problems involving converting between units of time. Use all four operations to solve problems involving measure using decimal notation including scaling.	Solve problems involving the calculation and conversion of units of measure, using decimal notation up to three decimal places where appropriate.
Geometry – properties of shapes					
Geometry – position and direction					
Statistics		Solve one-step and two-step questions using information presented in scaled bar charts and pictograms and tables.	Solve comparison, sum and difference problems using information presented in bar charts, pictograms, tables and other graphs.	Solve comparison, sum and difference problems using information presented in a line graph.	Interpret and construct pie charts and line graphs and use these to solve problems.

class dictionary on the working wall. Dictionaries of this type, which are developed by the children in response to their own learning needs, result in deeper understanding and better retention of technical terminology. As we saw above in the section on language, children should then be encouraged through paired discussion and group work to use the words they have learned and to share their understanding.

Critical questions

» What whole-school approaches to problem solving have you seen being implemented? Are there any potential barriers to effective problem solving, particularly with regard to representing problems, that exist over the different year groups of schools that you have experienced?

» Have you experienced successful whole-school approaches to developing the problem-solving abilities of children? What characteristics of these approaches made them successful?

Critical reflections

Let us now review and summarise the important issues that we have highlighted in this chapter on representing problems. Firstly, we have developed the ideas that we first introduced in the last chapter regarding the processes of problem solving, and have focussed specifically on the role of representing or reformulating the problem within the process. This notion of representing the problem is more complex than it might appear. It is not just a case of drawing a picture of a problem (for example, how would you represent a visual problem?). In making sense of a problem and finding a possible entry point into solving the problem, we might use concrete objects, we might use symbols, we might underline key words in a problem, we might indeed draw a picture, we might imagine or act out a problem situation, or we might draw on prior knowledge of similar problems that we have tackled before. We can see that this notion of representing can have quite a broad interpretation so, in examining how you and your children approach the teaching and learning of problem solving, we ask you to focus carefully on this part of the process and to consider how you can support children in this. We have provided some suggestions in this chapter but the key is to recognise the importance of this process yourself so that you have greater insight into how to support it.

It is interesting to note that in discussing the role of prior knowledge in representing problems, we have specifically not excluded the approach of practising different kinds of problems in order to develop children's knowledge for tackling problems. Having a particular approach to a problem is another representation that one can draw on. However, we have also emphasised the issue of functional fixedness and so, once again, in practising problems, placing the emphasis on how we might represent problems, rather than simply 'knowing' what to do in a given situation, will empower the children more in their problem solving.

Finally, we have touched upon the role played by language in representing problems, particularly in word problems. The language issue in mathematics teaching and learning is fascinating, but what we have emphasised here is that as a representation, it is open to interpretation by different people. This is true for all representations – what might be a useful representation for one child might not help another child to make sense of the problem. We have to acknowledge the complexity that this interpretation of language and other representations introduces, and find ways to support children. One way in which we can share, compare and examine our representations of problems (or any other concept for that matter) is through thorough discussion. Therefore, consider how discussion can meaningfully be incorporated into your teaching of problem solving, not just as a quick sharing of ideas for one minute between talk partners in the classroom, but as a meaningful reflection on the efficacy of different representations. We will move on in the next chapter to look further at the importance of this process of reflection.

Taking it further

From the psychological perspective of examining problem solving, not just within mathematics, Richard Mayer's textbook on *Thinking, problem solving, cognition* (1992) provides excellent detail. He also included a historical perspective on problem solving including the Gestalt view of thinking.

The paper by Pantziara, Gagatsis and Elia (2009), although complicated in places, provides good evidence for how the use of representations such as diagrams facilitates young children's problem solving in mathematics. More broadly, for those who are interested in exploring further the role of representations in the teaching and learning of mathematics, we refer to the paper by Pape and Tchoshanov (2001).

Mayer, R E (1992) *Thinking, problem solving, cognition*. WH Freeman/Times Books/Henry Holt & Co

Pantziara, M, Gagatsis, A, & Elia, I (2009) Using diagrams as tools for the solution of non-routine mathematical problems. *Educational Studies in Mathematics*, 72(1), 39–60

Pape, S J, & Tchoshanov, M A (2001) The role of representation(s) in developing mathematical understanding. *Theory into Practice*, 40(2), 118–127

4 Reasoning with problems

Key issues in this chapter

- This chapter begins by defining what we mean by 'reasoning' or 'thinking', and how this relates to what we do in mathematics.

- It shows that reasoning or thinking involves internally 'representing' the problem, linking back to the last chapter, and 'manipulating' this internal representation.

- It also demonstrates that an important part of the problem-solving process is reflecting upon this process of representing and manipulating, in other words 'thinking about our own thinking' or *metacognition*.

- Throughout, the chapter considers ways in which you can encourage children to reflect upon and improve their thinking or reasoning within the problem-solving process.

Introduction

Having examined in detail the importance of representing problems in the last chapter, we will now look in more detail at the importance of reflecting upon our progress towards a solution, and our approach to a problem. However, for reasons that will become clearer, we consider these issues under the title 'reasoning or thinking with problems'. The terms 'reasoning' or 'thinking' will be used interchangeably throughout the chapter in relation to mathematics. In the next section, we begin to define what we mean by these terms.

What do we mean by thinking or reasoning mathematically?

Whole volumes of philosophical, psychological and educational literature have been written on what is meant by 'thinking' or 'reasoning'. In some ways, this makes the job of defining what we mean by these terms more difficult. However, following the lead of Holyoak and Morrison (2005), let us start off with a definition in order to suggest where this could lead us:

Thinking is the systematic transformations of mental representations of knowledge to characterize actual or possible states of the world, often in service of goals.

(p.2)

Holyoak and Morrison's definition introduces a number of ideas which we need to explore more fully. Firstly, we come across the idea again of mental or internal representations of knowledge. In the last chapter, where we looked at the importance of 'representing' problems, we highlighted that, in order for us to know something, that something must be stored mentally in some way. Although we cannot directly access these, we refer to them as the internal or mental representation of the given concept.

Thinking or reasoning therefore involves some transformation of these mental representations. This view of thinking is very much in line with the mental models view of thinking put forward by Johnson-Laird (2005): *'Thinking, which enables us to anticipate the world and to choose a course of action, relies on internal manipulation of these mental models'* (p.185). Let us provide an example of what this transformation might look like. Here is a series of non-mathematical statements:

On a shopping trip, Lynn would like to shop for clothes or shop for shoes, but can't do both. Lynn could also go for a coffee if she shopped for clothes but not if she shopped for shoes because the shoe shop and coffee shop are too far away from each other. What are Lynn's options?

We could set up an initial mental model of the first two possibilities allowed. These might look like:

Shop for clothes   or   Shop for shoes

Then we might manipulate the mental model to match what else we could do:

Shop for clothes   or   Shop for shoes

Go for coffee

Therefore, Lynn can shop for clothes <u>and</u> go for a coffee, or shop for shoes. This is a simple example of setting up and manipulating a mental model. Obviously, the above example is an externalised representation in the form of written words, but we may develop a similar mental model in our minds. In terms of mathematical examples, we can look back at the last chapter to find possible examples of mental models that could be involved in our thinking. The sweets example that we gave may be similar to some internalised visual model for what we might have for the given problem. Alternatively, when we described the Tower of Hanoi problem, the set up involved in the Tower of Hanoi may become a mental model that we use to solve other isomorphic problems. What we are emphasising here is that, before we can think about or reason with a problem, we need to have an internal representation of the problem that we can work with. Once again, as we encountered in the last chapter, this emphasises the importance of representing or reformulating a problem.

What makes thinking mathematical?

Going back to the quote from Holyoak and Morrison, the other idea that it emphasises is that the thinking must involve *'systematic transformations'* of the mental models or representations. What might be meant by that? In reading the above description of thinking, one question that you may be asking is 'so what makes this mathematical?' It is this second requirement of systematic thinking that begins to move us to what we might more normally associate with mathematical thinking. Holyoak and Morrison explain further that these systematic transformations involve manipulations of the mental models that are governed by certain constraints. These constraints may be logical in nature, involving deductive reasoning where the conclusions drawn from the thinking process lead incontrovertibly from the starting premises. In mathematics, a great emphasis is placed on logical thinking and establishing proofs, and we may look for such systematic processes in children's thinking. However, we are not solely confined to deductive thinking. Holyoak and Morrison highlight creative 'leaps' in our thinking, where we might suddenly come up with a mental model that helps us to solve a problem. We will look further at creativity in the next chapter, but we emphasise here that our thinking may not be purely deductive – however, it must be systematic and cannot simply be unconstrained associations, such as might occur when we are initially brain storming. Once again, we will look further at this issue in the next chapter.

Here is an example that will provide further insight. In primary mathematics, you might consider the following questions with children:

Why does 7 × 3 give the same answer as 3 × 7?
Is it always true that you get the same answer when you swap numbers?

Now, what might young children's thinking be like with regards to the above? Some children may start off by investigating lots and lots of calculations involving multiplication of two numbers to see whether the latter statement seems to be true. Other children might simply state that the latter statement is true because their teacher had told them so. Yet other children may have a different mental model of multiplication involving an array (see Figure 4.1).

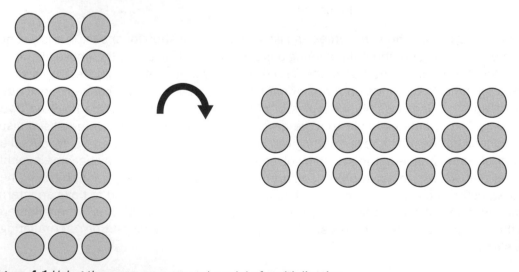

Figure 4.1 *Using the array as a mental model of multiplication*

Using this model, they might show that, since multiplication with two whole numbers can always be shown as an array, and the array can always be rotated as above, then two whole numbers multiplied together can always be swapped over to give the same result. What the above example illustrates is that in any given mathematical situation, children may exhibit different levels of thinking. Some children may be more logical than others. However, all the examples given above are examples of children's thinking, even though we may feel that some of the thinking is not very mathematical. In each case, whether it is collecting together lots of examples of calculations, or recalling from memory what the teacher said, or recalling a visual representation such as the array, children are building up or using their mental models associated with multiplication in order to tackle the questions.

Perspectives on mathematical thinking

In highlighting the different kinds of thinking that might be involved in mathematics, it is useful to recognise that we can look at thinking in two different ways. Mosely et al (2005) highlight that we can take a *psychological* or a *sociological* perspective on thinking. In the former, thinking *'is an internal, mental process that constructs and operates on mental representations of information'* (p.15), in line with the mental models view that we outlined above. However, we can also take a sociological perspective where the action of an individual *'relates to a wider society and the customs and practices that restrict and inhibit some behaviours and support and foster others'* (p.17). Therefore, when we talk about children 'thinking mathematically', the latter view implies that they are meeting the expectations of the mathematical discipline, where we aim to reason logically and deductively, in order to prove our assertions. Indeed, what we are often doing with children is trying to train them in the expectations of the subject. Therefore, as we have already highlighted in the above discussion, we need to be aware of these differing perspectives so that we can avoid any confusion about what we are trying to do when we talk about supporting children's mathematical thinking. Obviously when working with younger children, but equally applicable with children of any age, we need to take into account the types of thinking that children are carrying out (a psychological perspective), so that we can support them in moving to more logical and deductive thinking in their mathematics (a sociological perspective) as they develop.

To summarise, we already know that in problem solving an important part of the process is the representing of the problem to build up a mental model that we can work with. But when we are thinking, this involves, as we detailed before, the systematic manipulation of this mental model. Systematic can mean formally mathematical or it can involve less formal thinking. The manipulation of the mental model is of course inextricably linked with the representation of the problem, because we have to have a representation or model to start with. Therefore, thinking or reasoning encompasses both this building up of mental models and the manipulation of these models. We can relate this perspective more specifically to mathematical problem solving. Orton and Frobisher (1996) and Burton (1984) highlight the following kinds of processes as possibly being drawn upon by children in solving mathematical problems:

- *collecting information/data; ordering information/data; listing/tabulating/ recording; searching/observing patterns; noticing similarities/differences; exploring; extracting; breaking down the problem; guessing; trying cases; working backwards; predicting.*
- *reflecting upon data; checking; proving; generalising; explaining; talking; agreeing; questioning.*

In looking at the kinds of processes involved, it is possible to separate them into two categories. The top category of processes we would view as thinking or reasoning, involving the representing of the situation and the manipulation of this representation. So, when we collect data on a problem, we are beginning to represent the problem in a certain way and building up our mental model of the problem. When we are ordering the information, or extracting information, or even guessing solutions, we are trying to manipulate the representation and our mental model.

The bottom category, above, involves slightly different processes – processes that are more concerned with examining how we have carried out our thinking or reasoning. In reflecting or checking on our approaches, we are judging how well we have represented the problem and reasoned with the representations. In proving, again we are trying to establish that the conclusions lead deductively from the initial representations of the problem. In generalising, we are seeing whether our ways of thinking about the problem can be extended to different contexts. In explaining, talking, agreeing and questioning, we are justifying our ways of thinking or calling into question the thinking of others. Therefore, this latter category seems to involve processes where we are 'thinking about our thinking', or *metacognitive* processes, rather than just thinking. We will examine these kinds of processes shortly.

Critical questions

» *Reflect upon what you do when you think about a problem in mathematics, or in any other area for that matter. Can you describe exactly what you are doing? How does what you do compare with the idea of developing a mental model and manipulating this model?*

» *In your experience of teaching problem solving, how often are children actually developing their own thinking? If they are developing their own thinking, what classroom approaches support them in doing so? Alternatively, what might hinder children in this process of thinking?*

» *Is a psychological or a sociological view of mathematical thinking more useful for problem solvers of different ages or abilities? Or are they both important regardless of age?*

A LINK TO DATA HANDLING

However, before we examine metacognition, let us digress slightly for a moment in order to make an important connection between mathematical processes. Although this book is focussed specifically on problem solving, you might have noticed from the different mathematical processes highlighted above that they involve approaches that you might include and teach in data handling. For example, if you were carrying out a data-handling investigation with children, you would ask them to collect, order and tabulate information, look for patterns from the data collected and make inferences and predictions. In fact, we can make this link between problem solving and data handling more directly. Barmby et al (2009), drawing on different research that examined the processes involved, summarised the different aspects of data handling as follows.

- What shall we represent? – formulating the question.

- Representing the data – collecting, recording and organising the data.

- Reasoning with the data – analysing and interpreting the data; comparing data; predicting and inferring with the data.

- Reasoning about the data – looking behind the data at its collection.

When we carry out a data-handling exercise, we decide on our question to ask, and then we 'represent' the situation by collecting data on it. We then manipulate this representation by analysing the data in order to draw conclusions about the situation. Importantly as well, we reflect upon our data-handling process in order to examine whether the conclusions drawn are fully justified. In looking at data handling in this way, we hope it is clear that what we have just described is the same as the thinking/reasoning and metacognitive processes previously identified. In fact, if we consider problem solving as a more general process, then we see that data handling is simply part of that process. There is no need to consider data handling separately from problem solving. This connection between using data from real world contexts and problem solving is returned to in Chapter 7.

Critical questions

» *From your experience, in your teaching of data handling, how explicit are you with regards to the different stages of data handling? Are some stages highlighted more than others?*

» *Does the above link between data handling and problem solving seem reasonable?*

Thinking about our thinking

Returning now to the processes of 'thinking about our thinking' which we identified above, Mason et al (1985) places great importance on this process of reflecting on our answers to problems, and the thinking used to arrive at them. In fact, they argue, reflecting is the most important activity in the learning process because only when we have reflected on our experiences can we truly learn anything. Mason includes this process of reflection within a larger phase of the problem-solving process that he refers to as the 'review' phase. Indeed, many of the problem-solving process models that we looked at in Chapter 2 acknowledge that the process involves the ability to reflect upon one's own thinking. To quote Polya (1957) directly:

> *By looking back at the completed solution, by reconsidering and re-examining the result and the path that led to it, they could consolidate their knowledge and develop*

their ability to solve problems. A good teacher should understand and impress on his students the view that no problem whatever is completely exhausted. There remains always something to do; with sufficient study and penetration, we could improve any solution, and, in any case, we can always improve our understanding of the solution.

(pp.14–15)

This idea of developing understanding of the problem and the related mathematical topic is also highlighted by Dewey, cited in Hiebert et al (1996, p.15). Those who engage in reflection look for 'problems' in their approach to reaching a solution; in other words they *problematise* their thinking and solution methods. This act of problematising results in greater understanding for the solver.

Metacognition and self-regulation

This 'thinking about our thinking' is referred to as *metacognition*. Flavell (1976, cited in Mosely et al 2005, p.13) defines metacognition as knowledge about one's own cognitive processes. Similarly, Child (2004) defines metacognition as *'a person self-consciously examining his or her mental processes, becoming aware of problems and adjusting accordingly in order to improve effectiveness'* (p.161), which integrates the idea of problematising with reflecting. Mosely et al (2005) highlight that there is confusion between *metacognition* and *self-regulation*. A possible difference between the two is that metacognition involves the knowledge, skills and awareness required to reflect on our thinking. Self-regulation also includes motivation to do so. Nevertheless they both involve the process of reflecting upon our thinking and the process that we go through when problem solving. Schoenfeld (1992, p.355) summarises clearly this process of reflection:

'In the midst of intellectual activity ("problem solving", broadly construed), you kept tabs on how well things were going. If things appeared to be proceeding well, you continued along the same path; if they appeared to be problematic, you took stock and considered other options. Monitoring and assessing progress "on line", and acting in response to the assessments of on-line progress, are the core components of self-regulation.'

Schoenfeld in fact highlights that one of the key differences between expert and novice problem solvers is this ability to reflect upon one's approach to solving a problem. He provides an example of one pair of novice problem solvers who read a mathematical problem, try and tackle it, and stay with this approach even though they fail to make progress with the problem. They are unable to consider other ways of approaching the problem. This is contrasted with an expert problem solver, a mathematician, who spends much more time trying to understand a problem, not committing themselves to any one approach until they are confident, and explicitly making 'metacognitive' comments on how they are doing with the problem. Let us look at a particular problem in order to illustrate this 'on-line' monitoring of what we are doing when we try and solve the problem. We will use a visual problem as shown in Figure 4.2.

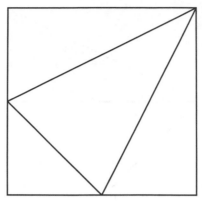

Figure 4.2 *What fraction is the middle isosceles triangle of the square? The base of the isosceles triangle touches the square at the centre of the square's sides.*

In engaging with the problem, you will be engaging in metacognitive processes straight away. You may be asking yourself 'What do I know in this problem?' Here, you are aware of trying to understand the problem more. Or you may think about how you can 'represent' the problem. For example you could split up the problem (Figure 4.3) using the fact that you notice a line of symmetry (applying your prior knowledge).

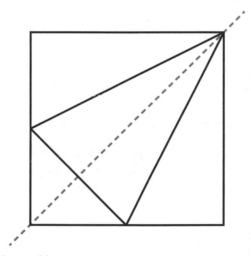

Figure 4.3 *Representing the problem*

But having done this, you may be asking yourself whether this is helpful? Is there a better way of dealing with the problem? You may notice now that although the new representation does not help directly, it does show that the top left right-angled triangle and the bottom right right-angled triangle are just reflections of each other, and that they can be combined. So let us try a new representation (Figure 4.4).

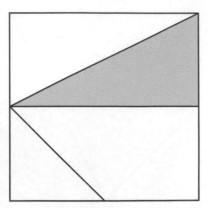

Figure 4.4 *Another representation*

When we move the bottom right right-angled triangle, we see that the two right-angled triangles cover half the square. And in fact, the smaller bottom left right-angled triangle is half of a quarter of the square – ie an eighth. Therefore the area outside the isosceles triangle is $\frac{1}{2}$ added to $\frac{1}{8}$ which is $\frac{5}{8}$. Therefore, the area of the isosceles triangle is the remainder of the whole square, ie $\frac{3}{8}$.

Now, although you have a solution, you might be thinking about how you can check this. If we say that the side of the square is of length 1 (so area 1), the sides of the bottom left-hand right-angled triangle are $\frac{1}{2}, \frac{1}{2}$ and $\frac{1}{\sqrt{2}}$ (using Pythagoras' theorem to find the third side). The base of the isosceles triangle is therefore $\frac{1}{\sqrt{2}}$. Likewise, the diagonal of the square is $\sqrt{2}$, and the height of the isosceles triangle is that diagonal take away half of the base of the isosceles triangle. Therefore, using ½ × base × height, the area of the isosceles triangle is:

$$\frac{1}{2} \times \frac{1}{\sqrt{2}} \times \left(\sqrt{2} - \frac{1}{2\sqrt{2}} \right) = \frac{1}{2} \times \left(1 - \frac{1}{4} \right) = \frac{1}{2} \times \frac{3}{4} = \frac{3}{8}$$

The area of the triangle is $\frac{3}{8}$ compared to the square which is 1. Happily, the two answers agree! Now you could consider if this was a better method (the first one is far more appropriate when working with primary children). You might also problematise the problem further and ask 'what would happen if the base of the isosceles triangle did not meet the middle of the square's sides?' So what would happen if they were a quarter of the way along (Figure 4.5)?

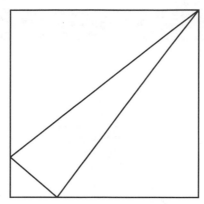

Figure 4.5 *Posing a new problem*

Can we see any pattern emerging as we pose this new problem and perhaps use any of our previous methods to solve this new problem? Can we try and generalise for this kind of problem?

By being metacognitively aware, we can continually monitor our progress when tackling the problem, and also extend the problem to try and further our understanding. In fact, you may have noticed that much of the metacognitive awareness highlighted in the above problem related directly to the problem-solving processes highlighted in this and the previous chapters. In fact, in specifying in detail what is involved in problem solving, what we are doing is trying to develop your metacognitive skills and knowledge, and in turn that of the children that you teach.

Developing metacognition

If metacognition is a key skill in problem solving, as highlighted by Mason above, then this leads us naturally to consider what we can do as teachers to develop children's metacognitive skills. Lester, Garofalo and Kroll (1989, cited in Schoenfeld, 1992, p.358) highlight a range of possible suggestions for teachers. We have arranged these suggestions in a way that draws attention to the different parts of the thinking process noted previously (see Figure 4.6 below). Firstly, there are suggestions that support children in the initial phase of coming up with understanding the problem, coming up with a representation for the problem and thinking through the problem (we would identify these suggestions with the first part of the problem-solving process highlighted by Orton and Frobisher (1996) and Burton (1984) above). Therefore, we have suggestions that deal with translating the language of the problem, as we highlighted in the previous chapter. Likewise, we have the idea of discussing the problem, to support this representing of the problem for children. In addition to supporting the representation of the problem, how we reason with the representations could be part of discussing the support for coming up with strategies. Of course, rather than the children sharing representations and strategies through discussion, the teachers themselves could provide ways of interpreting, representing and reasoning with problems through the use of hints.

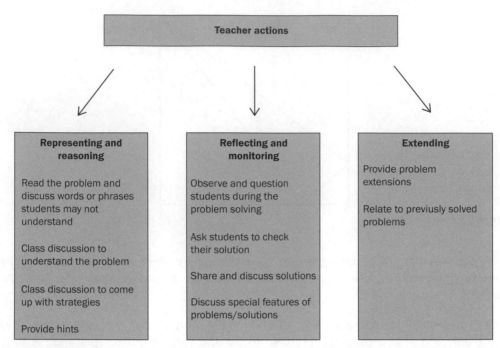

Figure 4.6 *Suggestions for developing children's metacognitive skills (from Lester, Garofalo and Kroll)*

The second and third categories of possible teacher actions are actions that we might more directly associate with 'metacognition' as a result of our previous discussion. In asking children to check how they have obtained their solutions to a problem, or in comparing different approaches that they have tried and highlighting particular aspects of their approaches, we are asking them to reflect on their thinking. We can more directly probe their thinking during the problem-solving process by observing what they do and questioning their approaches. Therefore, in the context of solving problems, here are possible questions that we might ask.

- Can you explain what you are doing? (Show me your thinking)

- Why have you done this? (Justify your thinking)

- How would you explain this to someone else? (Showing and justifying your thinking)

- Do you think this approach will always work? (Can you generalise/prove that your approach works)

- How else could you do this? (Extending your thinking)

- What happens if this changes? (Extending your thinking)

- Does this remind you of anything? (Extending your thinking)

We can see that the questions also move us to extend the children's thinking further, to problematise the question further or to encourage connections to other areas. Therefore, we can see that we can base our suggestions, for teaching related to problem solving and metacognition, directly on the elements of the problem-solving process that we have highlighted so far.

Critical questions

»   *Thinking about your own experiences of tackling mathematical problems, how aware are you of metacognitive processes that you carry out? Can you give some specific examples of these metacognitive processes? What supports you in developing these metacognitive processes?*

»   *In turn, what approaches have you seen or used in the classroom to develop children's metacognitive processes in problem solving? How successful have these been, and what constraints may occur in developing these processes in children?*

Reasoning with problems: the classroom perspective

An important point that we have emphasised above is that if children are to become proficient problem solvers they also need to be able to reason, to consider their own thinking, justify their choices and communicate these mathematically. This is often seen in schools to be a 'higher order maths skill' and so sometimes associated with the more able children, an assumption perhaps backed up by SAT papers where Level 5+ questions often ask for an explanation of an answer in order to gain the mark. Children who are not more able may struggle to clearly communicate their thinking in class and in test situations, and again this confirms a possible view that metacognition is something that mathematicians do, but mere mortals find difficult.

As an adult if you were asked the following questions, you would probably have little difficulty in coming up with an answer:

a)   15 + 16

b)   98 + 42

c)   61 – 58

But how easy would it be to explain how you came up with your answer? Take a moment to think about your own thinking. Did you use 'near doubles' for a) 15 + 15 + 1 = 31, partitioning for b) 98 + 2 + 40 = 140, and counting on for c) 58 + 2 + 1 = 61? You may have used other strategies, which is fine as long as they bring you to a correct answer and are efficient (ie have a minimal number of steps to reduce the opportunity to make mistakes). Using those same questions with children, teachers and other adults, however, it is surprising how often the only strategy available to calculate mentally is 'counting on in ones'. If this is the strategy you used throughout or if you used one other strategy for all of the questions you may just have learned something valuable about your own ability to calculate mentally.

If this is a useful exercise to assess proficiency in the use of mental calculation strategies and in practising metacognition for adults, would similar activities not be useful in the classroom? Children could write down their thought processes next to each calculation or could sort calculations into groups relating to a particular mental strategy. They may find this activity quite difficult to begin with if they have not been taught to communicate their reasoning, but it is worth persevering. A similar activity, sorting problems into types rather than solving them, encourages children to consider different problem types, think about the process of problem solving, reflect upon their prior knowledge and reason mathematically without the pressure of having to find an answer.

In many educational establishments we do not explicitly teach or train children how to think about their thinking, but we ask children the type of questions illustrated earlier:

* Can you explain what you are doing?

* Why have you done this?

* How would you explain this to someone else?

We also expect that, by asking frequently, children will come to realise what we expect as an answer. However, an effective way to facilitate thinking about thinking in the classroom is to use the model proposed by Sue Waring from the Mathematical Association in her publication *Can You Prove It?* (2005):

Making progress in communicating ideas, orally and in writing

Stage 1: Convince yourself (mental justification)

Stage 2: Convince a friend (oral justification)

Stage 3: Convince a pen friend (informal written justification)

Stage 4: Convince your teacher (formal written justification)

Ideally this process begins in Key Stage 1 and develops through Key Stage 2, although we ourselves have seen great improvements in children's reasoning and communication skills by simply building this model into teaching across Year 6. Developing their skills progressively in this way empowers children of all abilities to reason mathematically.

As we highlighted earlier, reasoning should also be seen as reflecting on the process of problem solving while actually engaged in the activity, as well as considering one's own mathematical route taken to a solution. Children who work in groups, representing the problem, discussing strategies and sharing ideas, are much more likely to find an access point, break the problem into steps and come to a conclusion. The problem with group work though is that the more able children may take over and 'do' the maths for the less able. So how, as educators, do we balance the benefits of group work with the drawbacks? One solution is to give each child in the group a specific role, eg:

Organiser: makes sure everyone in the group:

* has a task to do;

* understands the task;

- has the opportunity to ask questions or offer solutions.

Recorder: makes sure that:

- all ideas and reasoning are recorded;
- all representations are recorded;
- the team contribute to a reflective report at the end.

Manager: makes sure:

- everyone has the resources they need to complete the task;
- all calculations are checked.

Coordinator: makes sure:

- everyone understands;
- each team member can explain their reasoning at the end of the task.

This allows each child to participate fully in the activity and, while carrying out their role, they are reasoning about the group problem-solving process. Upon completion of the activity, it is useful to 'mix up' the groups to allow children to explain their mathematical thinking and to communicate their reasoning to others. For example:

- two people from each group move to join a different group;
- the two 'hosts' explain their findings to the two 'visitors';
- the 'visitors' act as critical friends, encouraging clear mathematical explanations, justifications and reasoning;
- the 'visitors' then share anything they did differently within their own group.

This links with stage 2 of the 'convince' scenario mentioned above.

Critical questions

» *From your experience, have you seen any whole-school approaches to developing the mathematical thinking of children? Are different approaches used or emphasised for problem solvers at different stages of learning?*

Critical reflections

To conclude this chapter, let us reflect upon the thinking that we have carried out in this chapter. What we have tried to do is to show that, in addition to 'representing' the problem which we highlighted in the last chapter, an additional key part of the problem-solving process is to reason or think about the problem. This includes reflecting upon and evaluating the approaches we take in tackling the problem. In fact, in defining what we mean by thinking, what we have shown is that this includes the process of representing. We can therefore say that this process of thinking or reasoning is the key process involved in problem solving.

Clarifying this notion of thinking, and relating it to problem solving, has powerful implications for what we do in the classroom. Firstly, it allows us to be clearer about this notion of 'mathematical thinking'. It is easy for educators to talk about developing children's mathematical thinking but, in actually trying to clarify this notion, we can start to see how exactly this fits into our teaching. In reading this chapter, you may have been thinking that, for most of the suggestions, you 'do that anyway'. You ask pupils to explain their methods, to discuss their approaches with each other, to share their solution approaches. However, what we hope you have got out of this chapter is a clearer appreciation of why you do these things, particularly in the context of problem solving.

The second implication for practice is that we start to appreciate that pupils are often involved in 'mathematical thinking', even if we sometimes view their thinking as not being very mathematical. Even with younger pupils, they are developing their ways of thinking, and one of our jobs as teachers of mathematics is to encourage them in reflecting upon their thinking, so that thinking can become more mathematical. Therefore, when observing your pupils as they engage in mathematical activities, look for opportunities to access their thinking, so that you can support them in their development of this thinking. Of course, we already do this, through our questioning, through asking for explanations, through the sharing of solutions in the classroom. Once again, through the considerations that we have made in the chapter, we can be clearer about what we are doing in the classroom.

The final implication that we highlight is that in emphasising thinking or reasoning as the key process in problem solving, in fact in doing mathematics generally, we are moving the emphasis from getting the correct answer to considering how we obtained that solution. In Chapter 8, we will suggest that this simple change in emphasis, ie to concentrating on children's thinking in mathematics, will result in far greater engagement with the mathematics by the pupils. What we emphasise here is that this simple change in our view of mathematics will have a powerful impact on the classroom. As Burton (1984, p.9) emphasised:

> *'Mathematics is a doing subject ... Mathematics is used to solve useful problems; it can be played with in a creative way to see what can be discovered; it is the basis on which amusing puzzles can be invented; it has a great power to inform. But they are not the best reasons. The greatest value of this approach is in the effect it has in the classroom.'*

Indeed, in the next chapter, we will explore this additional issue of creativity and problem solving.

Taking it further

Leone Burton's book *Thinking things through: Problem solving in mathematics* (1984) is a seminal book on problem solving and is well worth a read. An interesting overview of the thinking process is provided by Mosely et al (2005). For a more general view of thinking, and in particular more detail on the mental models of thinking outlined in this chapter, we recommend Philip Johnson-Laird's writings.

For a more specific look at mathematical thinking and ways of developing mathematical thinking in the primary school, Burton's 1984 journal paper goes into good detail on this issue.

Burton, L (1984) Mathematical thinking: the struggle for meaning. *Journal for Research in Mathematics Education*, 15(1), 35–49

Burton, L (1984) *Thinking things through: problem solving in mathematics*. Oxford: Blackwell

Johnson-Laird, P N (1983) *Mental models: towards a cognitive science of language, inference, and consciousness*. Cambridge: Cambridge University Press

Mosely, D, Baumfield, V, Elliott, J, Gregson, M, Higgins, S, Miller, J, & Newton, D P (2005) *Frameworks for thinking: a handbook for teaching and learning*. Cambridge: Cambridge University Press

5 Creativity and problem solving

Key issues in this chapter

- This chapter makes the connection between the idea of creativity, and the problem-solving process in mathematics. Although creativity is not always closely associated with the study of mathematics, we hope to show that it is integral to problem solving.

- It clarifies this link between problem solving and creativity by specifying exactly what is meant by creativity. It shows that the creative process involves identifying new connections and approaches, but also that these connections and approaches are useful. It makes explicit links to the metacognitive processes discussed in the last chapter.

- In addition to problem solving as a creative process, the idea of problem posing, which is also often associated with creativity, is introduced. Problem posing by both the teacher and the child are shown as integral to developing the problem-solving approach.

- The importance of creativity and mathematics is emphasised by making the link between creativity and mathematical ability and understanding. Having emphasised this importance, specific suggestions for fostering creativity in the classroom are put forward.

Introduction

Previous chapters have discussed the precise nature of problem solving. This chapter explores a concept not often associated with mathematics – creativity. It explores the nature of creativity, what it looks like in the mathematics classroom, the role that it can play in the act of problem solving and problem posing, and how it might be encouraged in children.

Research tells us that mathematics is seldom a subject associated with the act of creativity (Pehkonen, 1997; Davies et al, 2004; Bolden et al, 2010), and is often low in the list of school subjects described as such (Newton, 2012). Creativity in mathematics was often viewed in the past as the domain of extraordinary and gifted individuals who could produce new knowledge or a new way of doing things (Weisberg, 1988; Sternberg, 1988; Gruber and Wallace, 2000). This has been termed 'the genius' or 'big C' view of mathematical creativity (Csikszentmihalyi, 1996). More recently however, there has developed a more 'egalitarian' notion of creativity. This notion views a creative act as one that is new to the *self* and therefore allows for the possibility that everyone is capable of creative activity to some degree. This might be termed the 'little c' view of creativity (eg see Craft, 2003; Boden, 2004).

Others too accept that children sitting in mathematics classrooms are capable of creative thinking in mathematics (Sriraman, 2005; 2008). Consequently, this view of creativity is one which is relevant to the teaching of mathematics to young children, in any number of simple classroom scenarios. For example, children are being creative in mathematics when they discover or derive a new number fact from an already known number fact, such as when a child spots and uses the proximity of 5 + 6 to the known number fact of 5 + 5 = 10, or when a child realises that a number can be partitioned in many different ways other than just in the place value format, eg that 12 can be partitioned canonically into 10 + 2 but in other ways too, 8 + 4 or 6 + 6.

Although teachers of primary-aged children often claim to believe that the mathematics in their classrooms is creative, closer inspection of that practice often suggests that it is not. Instead, what the teachers seem to be referring to is the opportunities their mathematics sessions provide for *creative teaching*, such as the creative use of resources and activities, rather than *teaching for creative thought* in children (Worthington and Carruthers, 2003; Carruthers and Worthington, 2005). In fact, much research from around the world suggests that the current way in which the teaching of mathematics is approached only serves to stifle creativity (Kennedy, 2005; Mann, 2006; Skiba et al, 2010; Bolden et al, 2010), and creativity can sometimes be viewed as an unwanted distraction from the aim of the lesson (Beghetto, 2007).

Such views are not only linked to the tendency of teachers to think of creativity as *teaching creatively*, but also with teachers' tendencies to conceive of mathematics as more of a *convergent* rather than a *divergent* activity, ie that the aim of many mathematics lessons is the search for the one and only correct answer. We view mathematical creativity, instead, as being closely linked with deep and flexible content knowledge, divergent thinking, problem solving, problem posing and the process of reflection. We will shortly discuss these issues in greater detail.

Critical questions

» *In the past, if you have referred to creativity in mathematics or in any other subject, how have you thought about the notion of creativity? Have you considered it more from a child or a teacher perspective?*

» *If you were to look at your own practice critically, on the whole, how often would you say you approach the teaching of mathematics from a divergent perspective? What constraints have you experienced in terms of introducing divergent activities?*

What then is creativity?

In the above discussion, we have started to get some insight into what we mean by creativity, and will explore this issue more now. We have already seen that the concept of creativity is a complex one. In fact, Treffinger et al (2002) have identified over 100 different definitions. However, as we have seen already, a common theme from the research is that creativity is a personal activity intended to produce something new. For instance, Bergström (1984) defines creativity as *'performance where the individual is producing something new and unpredictable'* (as cited by Pehkonen, 1997, p. 159). Kwon, Park and Park (2006, p. 52) define creativity as a *'high-dimensional human ability or skill to think up something new'*.

However, the idea of creating something new is not the only aspect to creativity. Other definitions of creativity emphasise that the 'product' of the creative process must be 'useful' as well. For example, *'Creativity is the ability to produce work that is original, but still appropriate and useful.'* (Woolfolk et al, 2008, p.366). Likewise, a report by The National Advisory Committee on Creative and Cultural Education (NACCCE, 1999) emphasised that the creative process involved evaluation and reflection of the product and the process; not just at the end of the process, but during it as well. Therefore, we suggest that a useful way of thinking about creativity is in terms of creating something new, making a connection to a new way of thinking or finding a new approach, but at the same time, evaluating the usefulness of this creative approach.

Critical question

» *How does the above view of creativity fit with your approach to thinking creatively? For example, taking a creative approach such as brain storming, do you incorporate both connecting to new ideas and also reflecting upon these ideas?*

Creativity and problem solving

So how does creativity link in with problem solving? It has been identified in the research that problem solving, and also something we call 'problem posing', is closely linked with creative activity in mathematics (Haylock, 1987; Silver, 1997). We will look at problem posing shortly. But why is problem solving so closely linked to creativity? We can answer this question by going back to our problem-solving processes. When we problem solve, we 'represent' the problem in a different way. Now if we are well practiced with the kind of problem presented to us, this way of thinking about the problem may be a familiar one (and perhaps the problem is not much of a problem after all). But if the problem is not so familiar, we may need to develop a new way of thinking about it. Or, we choose to actively try and find a new way of thinking about a problem (perhaps by representing the problem in a way we may not have tried). In the last chapter, when we looked at the triangle in the square and worked out what fraction the triangle was of the square, we were doing just this. But in addition to trying to find a new way of thinking about the problem, we were also reflecting on the usefulness of our approach. Just because an approach to a problem is new, it does not mean it is necessarily useful, or better than approaches we had tried before. We can see that, according to the view of creativity given above, this is mirrored closely by the processes we carry out in problem solving. Therefore, we argue that genuine problem-solving activities by their very nature involve creativity on the part of the problem solver. However, being flexible in problem solving is by no means the only way of being mathematically creative. Being allowed opportunities to pose problems can also lead to children showing their mathematical creativity (Silver, 1997). We examine this issue of problem posing next.

Problem posing as creativity

The ability to pose problems has also traditionally been identified as an indicator of exceptional ability in mathematics (Hadamard, 1954; Balka, 1974; Burton, 1998). More generally though, we argue that problem posing in a variety of senses can improve children's ability to problem solve. However, in trying to understand what we mean by problem posing, Silver (2013) asks the question *'problem solving by whom and for what purpose?'* (p.159). Let us also explore this question so we can understand a little more about this additional process associated with creativity.

Problem posing by children

Firstly, children themselves or those trying to solve a given problem can ask questions of themselves about the problem. This creates opportunities: for reasoning through the problem-solving approach, to extend their thinking and make creative links to other areas of mathematics, to open up new avenues or conjectures about how to approach a problem, and also to communicate this to others. These processes of questioning how we are approaching the problem, to *problematise* what we are doing, to reflect upon our approach, is part of the metacognitive processes discussed in the last chapter. Therefore, we can see how the act of problem posing is integral to the overall problem-solving process. In turn, we can see once again how creative approaches are aligned to that of problem solving. The research tells us too that opportunities that allow children to problematise their mathematics can improve understanding and problem-solving abilities (Hiebert et al, 1996). In devising a programme to develop children's mathematical creativity, Sheffield (2009) suggests that children should be encouraged to extend their mathematical explorations by asking questions concerning *who* (who can restate this in their own words), *what* (what patterns/generalisations do I see?), *when* (when does this work or not work?), *where* (where could I go next?), *why* (why does that work?) and *how* (how does this relate to real life?). Recent work suggests that children trained in such techniques not only strengthen their mathematical creativity but also improve their general mathematical abilities compared to children not trained (Sheffield, 2009).

Problem posing by the teacher

Another view of problem posing might be that problem posing is carried out by the teacher. This may be the 'straightforward' act of generating problems for children to solve. Or, it may be questioning the problem-solving process carried out by the children. Following on from the previous view of problem posing and its relation to metacognition, the teacher can also help in this process by using questioning that is open-ended rather than closed, ie questioning which demands that children go beyond the answer and demonstrate their reasoning (Sheffield, 2009). For example, referring back to the last chapter on reasoning and problem solving, we saw that recommendations for developing chldren's metacognitive abilities in problem solving included the teacher questioning chldren's thinking throughout the solution process, and also encouraging them to make connections to new areas. Therefore, once again, problem posing is very much part of the problem-solving process, incorporating the role of the teacher as well.

Posing completely new problems

There is another view of problem posing that is very much related to the previous point made. We can view problem posing in the sense of the children generating new problems themselves. This may be carried out after the successful completion of the original problem, posing related problems in order to extend their thinking. Or, the problem solver might pose these problems for themselves earlier on in tackling a problem situation. For example, looking ahead at the coming chapter when we examine other 'open approaches' to mathematics, we will see that in order to make such an open situation more manageable in terms of tackling it (for example a more open investigation in mathematics), we need to decide exactly what question or questions we want to try and answer. Therefore, from this perspective as well, the act of problem posing is integral to the broader problem-solving process. And the fact that the problem solvers themselves are formulating new questions about a situation links us back to the creative process, although the consideration of whether a question posed is in fact useful, or whether a better question could instead be posed, must remain part of the process too. It will hopefully be clear when we discuss these open approaches to mathematics that when we refer to creative approaches to tackling such open situations, we can understand why we link such situations with creativity.

Critical questions

»   *When you are tackling mathematical problems, do you use any aspects of problem solving? If so, in what way?*

»   *Have you come across or supported yourself the explicit use of problem posing in the mathematical classroom? If so, in what manner? Was this problem posing by the teacher or the children?*

Creativity as an indicator of mathematical ability

In the discussion so far on creativity, we hope that we have established clearly this link between creativity and problem solving, incorporating the idea of problem posing as well. We hope it is clear that, in considering the processes involved in problem solving, if we take a particular view of creativity, this view is implicit in the processes we have discussed so far. Interestingly, in developing the idea of this close link between creativity and problem solving, we should note that, in the past, the act of creativity has been seen as an indicator of mathematical ability, in particular where mathematical ability itself has usually been measured in terms of a child's ability to solve problems (Haylock, 1987). Specifically, mathematical ability has been measured using the extent to which a child can show *flexibility*, *fluency* and *originality* in their problem solving, or indeed in their problem posing (Guilford, 1967; Torrance, 1974). Flexibility can be measured by children's ability to use a variety of different methods or approaches to the problem (or by posing problems that can be solved in different ways); fluency can be measured by the number of appropriate solutions produced (or by posing a number of different problems); and originality can be measured by the relative novelty of those responses (or by posing problems that are different from the one previously solved) (Haylock, 1987; Silver, 1997). In fact, researchers such as Haylock have used these ideas around flexibility, fluency and originality as a basis for assessing children's creativity in mathematical problem solving. We will look further at the issue of assessing problem-solving abilities in the next chapter.

We can go further in exploring this close relationship between problem solving, child creativity, and child ability in mathematics. We saw in the introduction to this book that it was the Cockroft report in the UK (Cockroft, 1982) which re-established problem solving as the heart of effective learning and teaching of mathematics, although many researchers had never swayed from that belief. The Cockroft report was commissioned by the UK government at the time as a result of concerns that young children were not developing the necessary mathematical skills and understandings, especially in mental calculation, and that teachers were relying too heavily on published schemes in their teaching. The report argued that *'the ability to solve problems is at the heart of mathematics'* (Cockcroft, 1982, p. 249), and so it included in its list of recommendations that problem solving be better integrated into the primary mathematics curriculum.

Creativity and understanding

This official recognition of problem solving as central to the effective learning and teaching of mathematics would have been warmly welcomed by those researchers who had long been advocates of using a child's problem-solving ability as a measure of mathematical creativity (eg Guilford, 1967; Torrance, 1974). Children's ability to show 'divergent' thinking when presented with mathematical problems was their criteria for creativity. Divergent thinking is often neglected in mathematics classrooms; instead there is too often a focus on learning specific skills and procedures where the main aim is to indentify the one and only solution to a given problem, ie convergent thinking.

Despite the tendency for mathematics to be viewed as a subject with a set body of knowledge – where algorithms and the search for 'the right answer' are paramount – what the research on divergent thinking suggests is that being creative is an important part of developing understanding in mathematics. We can see this by making the distinction between procedural and conceptual understanding in mathematics. Procedural understanding relates to the extent to which children show computational accuracy, whereas conceptual knowledge is characterised by an understanding of how and why those computations work. This dichotomy is also reflected in Polya's (1957) distinction between mathematical *information* and mathematical *know how* respectively. A child can solve a mathematical problem by correctly applying a learned algorithm without having any real conceptual understanding of how that answer came to be. Having some degree of conceptual understanding alongside the procedural competence allows the child much greater scope to show their mathematical creativity. In developing our understanding of mathematics (and of any subject for that matter), what is also necessary is the ability to break free from the established way of doing things and to apply this sound knowledge base in order to see opportunities beyond the given (Krutetskii,

1976; Cropley, 1992; Haylock, 1997; Sriraman, 2008). That is, the combination of being able to break free from the usual way of doing things (see Mayer's functional fixedness in Chapter 3), and being able to show flexibility in one's approach to problem solving, is where the understanding of mathematics lies. Therefore, we can appreciate this close link between problem solving, creativity, and mathematical ability or understanding.

Let us illustrate this with an example. Most teachers are likely to have experienced children showing fixation at some point or another, as when they try to use a previously learned algorithm to complete a problem when the algorithm is not the best choice of approaches. A particular example comes from the National Numeracy Project, which was set up in the UK in 1996 (Straker, 1999). One of the arithmetic problems it used to assess children's ability to calculate mentally was 3000 – 1997. Surprisingly, only 31% of the 10 year olds involved in the project answered this question correctly. A subsequent analysis of the children's attempts at this question revealed that many of them failed because they were attempting to use the traditional vertical algorithm for subtraction, when it would have been easier to use a more informal approach, eg counting on mentally or using a number line. That is, the failure was due to the children's fixation on a previously learned algorithm, even when it was inappropriate. Once again, in solving any given problem and demonstrating their mathematical ability, what is required is not simply a convergent approach to the problem, but a divergent view where other perhaps more effective approaches to solving the problem are considered. We can therefore see how mathematical creativity is closely linked to ability in the subject.

Fostering creativity in the mathematics classroom

Teachers in the UK (and in other countries) are increasingly being encouraged to offer children problem solving and creative experiences in mathematics (NACCCE, 1999; Ofsted, 2008; DfES, 2003; DfES/DCMS, 2006). However, there appears to be a dearth of information concerning how teachers might encourage children to be creative and use real problem-solving skills and strategies (Makel, 2009). We hope the information given throughout this book will go some way in supporting teachers to *teach creatively* and to *teach for creativity* in mathematics. The following section will attempt to provide some more specific suggestions.

Fluency, flexibility and originality

The discussion above concerning Guildford's (1967) distinction between convergent and divergent thinking suggests that children should be encouraged to develop their mathematical creativity by being offered activities which are open-ended and have multiple solutions. Kwon et al (2006) developed a programme aimed at encouraging divergent thinking in primary-aged children via open-ended tasks, and discovered that their use was indeed helpful in developing mathematical creativity (as measured by *fluency, flexibility* and *originality*). In Chapter 7, we will detail possible open-ended approaches to mathematics that could be used. We note here that considering the use of such approaches may cause some difficulties for teachers as encouraging divergent thinking requires them to have confidence in their own mathematical ability and to break away from the usual way of doing things, ie using closed or convergent problems. It also requires time, something which teachers seem to lack (see Bolden and Newton, 2008). However, we reiterate that only by providing children with open-ended problem-solving opportunities can we hope to develop children's fluency, flexibility, and originality in problem solving, and thus the ability to break free from established mindsets (Haylock, 1987; Silver, 1997; Mann, 2006).

Developing creative thinking

We have also seen how allowing children to problem pose as well as problem solve are ways in which children can be encouraged to develop their mathematical creativity. In relation to this, it is important to note that developing an appropriate classroom ethos is crucial to encouraging young children's creativity in mathematics. An ethos where questioning by children as well as the teacher and risk-taking, in terms of looking for new approaches to problems, are encouraged, and where mistakes are viewed as potential pathways to greater understanding rather than outcomes to be avoided at all costs, will help greatly in this respect. The list below offers you some general principles for developing creative thinking in your children.

* Question your own approach to mathematics; ie can it be creative or is it about memorising rules?

* Empower the learner, for example by encouraging a 'have a go' ethos in your classroom where mistakes/misconceptions are embraced as teaching and learning opportunities, by involving them at times in deciding on the mathematics to be learned, by asking them to problem pose not just to problem solve.

* Allow some opportunities for children to 'discover' the mathematics, rather than always setting out the learning objective at the beginning of the lesson.

* Embrace 'open-endedness', eg use more open-ended problems with multiple solutions rather than closed problems (see Chapter 7), and use more open-ended questions which require children to think about their answer rather than closed questions that requires a closed response, eg yes/no or definitive answer.

* Encourage children to reason through their ideas and answers. Use the '*who, what, when, where, why, how*' approach.

Developing metacognition and reflection

In particular, this last aspect of developing childrens metacognitive thinking when tackling problems will allow, through problem posing, for more creative thinking to take place in the mathematics classroom. For example, going back to the mental calculations from the last chapter, we can simply reflect on the strategies used upon completion of these calculations. We might have used the following strategies:

a) $15 + 16 = 10 + 10 + 5 + 5 + 1$ (add tens, then units, partitioning into '5 and a bit')

b) $98 + 42 = 90 + 10 + 40$ (find complements to 10 and 100)

c) $61 - 58 = 61 - 60 + 2$ (round up and adjust)

In order to support reflections, and going back to the role that discussion can play in the problem-solving process given in Chapter 3, discussion with a partner or within a group can help children to evaluate the strategies they have used, to help them think about their own and others' thinking, and to explore different ways of tackling the problem. Even doing this as an adult, looking back, it is easy to see where you might have used a more efficient method, although 'efficiency' is not the only criteria we could use to judge our methods. Reflecting upon strategies used helps to embed learning and understanding and offers the opportunity to explore alternative and more creative strategies. Reflection and adaptation should be acknowledged as part of the mathematical process; we have seen that, in terms of the broader problem-solving process, they are more important goals for producing competent problem solvers than 'finding a solution'.

Let us provide an additional, more specific, suggestion to support children in their metacognitive reflections. Concept cartoons are a simple but effective way of sharing strategies for children to discuss, and are also a particularly useful tool to promote discussion, hypothesising, reasoning and reflection when problem solving. For example, we have produced the concept cartoon in Figure 5.1, related to the problem given in that figure.

Figure 5.1 *An example of a concept cartoon to encourage creativity in children's problem solving*

Concept cartoons allow children to discuss alternative strategies and solutions while distancing themselves from right and wrong answers. They encourage creative thought and open up the world of 'different paths to the same route'. Although they allow children of all abilities to enter into the same discussion, they are not a replacement for developing the 'have a go' ethos; rather they are a complement to it. We need children to realise that if the method to a solution was immediately apparent, it would be an exercise not a problem. We need to give them opportunities to practise accessing problems, to develop their ability to persevere, and to realise that you learn something even if you are not on the right path to a solution. Making mistakes is a valid part of problem solving and should not be regarded as failure. Failure is when you give up. As Einstein said, *'it's not that I'm so smart, it's just that I stay with problems longer'*.

Concept cartoons can be used alongside stepping stone problems to develop children's abilities in creative thinking. Stepping stones should be introduced in a progressive manner.

Stage 1: Use the first problem as a stepping stone to solving the second.

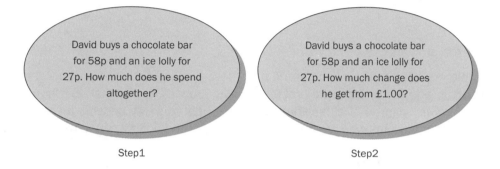

David buys a chocolate bar for 58p and an ice lolly for 27p. How much does he spend altogether?

Step1

David buys a chocolate bar for 58p and an ice lolly for 27p. How much change does he get from £1.00?

Step2

Stage 2: Provide children with the question they must ask first.

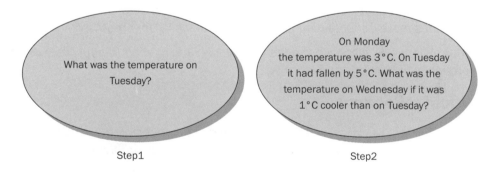

What was the temperature on Tuesday?

Step1

On Monday the temperature was 3°C. On Tuesday it had fallen by 5°C. What was the temperature on Wednesday if it was 1°C cooler than on Tuesday?

Step2

Stage 3: Ask the children to decide on the question which must be answered first.

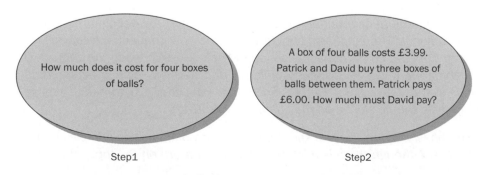

How much does it cost for four boxes of balls?

Step1

A box of four balls costs £3.99. Patrick and David buy three boxes of balls between them. Patrick pays £6.00. How much must David pay?

Step2

Stepping stones help children to break problems down into manageable chunks, improving accessibility. We will see how this 'stepping stone' method is required for more open-problem situations in Chapter 7.

In settings where problem solving is at the heart of mathematics education, teachers develop these kinds of activities and they are integral to creative thinking. For example, instead of teaching children key words and phrases as a tool to support understanding, a creative teacher will encourage children to use these words and phrases to pose their own problems:

Your phrase is:

How many more do they need?

Your answer is 15.

What is the problem?

Good problem-solving schools understand that these types of activities encourage children to take part in and learn about the problem-solving process, rather than just trying to find a correct answer. Children of all abilities who are taught this way become more confident, reflective mathematicians who are willing to 'have a go', and not give up at the first hurdle.

Critical questions

» *Have you experienced any whole-school approaches to encouraging creativity, in particular in mathematics? What approaches to creativity were introduced, and which approaches did you feel were more successful? Once again, were the approaches more about teaching creatively or teaching for creativity?*

» *In your experience, what constraints do schools face in encouraging creative approaches to teaching and learning?*

Critical reflections

In this chapter, we hope we have convinced the reader of the close connections between thinking creatively in mathematics, and the problem-solving processes that we have discussed in this book. And let us emphasise again that what we are focussing on is children thinking creatively, not just teachers teaching mathematics in a creative way. Very often, if one asks schools to show examples of creativity in the classroom, they may show beautiful wall displays, or cross-curricular approaches to mathematics. Now, although these may lead to children making new connections to their mathematical understanding, and therefore by definition creative thinking, they may not. The emphasis should be on the new connections that children make rather than the new approaches taken by the teacher to teach the subject. Of course, teaching creatively can engage children and develop their understanding through their own creative links. But we encourage teachers just to bear in mind that the emphasis should still be on the children's creativity.

In emphasising this, we can see the role that problem posing can play in this creative process. Although there is a lot of research literature on the topic of problem posing in the teaching and learning of mathematics, explicit reference to problem posing in the classroom is, in our experience, not so common. We hope that explicitly thinking about how to incorporate problem posing into your own teaching, and encouraging problem posing by the children that you work with, will enhance your teaching of mathematics and your own creativity, engaging not only the children but you as well! Having underlined the importance of focussing on children thinking creatively in the classroom, we do acknowledge that there is a close connection between teachers' and children's creativity, and focussing on one will most likely impact on the other. We hope that you, too, are engaged by the process of incorporating creativity into the classroom particularly through problem solving and problem posing.

Taking it further

The fields of both creativity in general and mathematical creativity in particular are huge but the teacher interested in applying some of the principles discussed above in their classroom should look at Leikin et al's edited book. It is full of chapters offering useful insight into all things creative.

To show the close link between creativity and problem solving from a research perspective, we recommend Silver (1997) who has written extensively on mathematics and creativity, including problem posing.

From a more practical perspective, with examples of how creativity can be incorporated into the classroom (and not just in terms of mathematics), we recommend the NACCCE report that can be downloaded from the internet.

In terms of problem posing, in addition to the writings of Silver, the short paper by Stoyanova and Ellerton provides a perspective from the classroom with younger secondary pupils.

Leikin, R, Berman, A & Koichu, B (eds.) (2009) *Creativity in mathematics and the education of gifted students* (pp. 87–100). Rotterdam: Sense Publishers

Silver, E A (1997) Fostering creativity through instruction rich in mathematical problem solving and problem posing. *ZDM*, 29(3), 75–80

Stoyanova, E, & Ellerton, N F (1996) A framework for research into students' problem posing in school mathematics, in Clarkson, P C (ed), *Technology in mathematics education* (pp. 518–525). Mathematics Education Research Group of Australasia. The University of Melbourne

NACCCE (1999) *All our futures: creativity, culture and education*. London: DfEE

6 Assessing problem solving

Key issues in this chapter

- This chapter sheds light on how you might go about assessing children as they tackle problem solving (and other open approaches to mathematics). Ofsted has recently highlighted the difficulties encountered by teachers, particularly student teachers, which emphasises the importance of this issue.

- It begins by discussing ways which we feel are insufficient for assessing problem-solving skills – for example simply looking at right or wrong answers to so-called 'real-life' problems that require a particular interpretation by children.

- It then discusses other possible approaches for assessment highlighted by the research, before relating these approaches specifically to problem-solving processes that have been highlighted in this book. Based on these processes, it proposes an approach to assessment which is closely related to classroom approaches to assessment.

Introduction

The previous chapters of the book have gone into a great deal of detail on the problem-solving process, including the links to the idea of creativity and other open approaches to mathematics. However, one key area not touched upon so far, which is essential in a book for teachers, is how problem solving can be assessed in schools. In a recent Ofsted report on good practice in Initial Teacher Education with regards to primary mathematics (Ofsted, 2013), a particular area of improvement identified by the inspectorate was the planning and assessing of problem solving and application of mathematics in real-life contexts. Therefore, this chapter specifically tackles the issue of assessment of problem solving, which in turn can be applied to other open approaches to mathematics, which are tackled in the next chapter. This is done by referring back to the processes involved in problem solving that have been discussed so far. Firstly, the issue of why assessment should be a difficulty for teachers and trainees is examined.

The difficulty of assessing problem solving

In a recent research paper looking at why open approaches such as investigations are not being used so much in today's primary classrooms, Sangster (2012) identified the fact that open-ended activities are difficult to assess. This is because, by definition, as we saw in the last chapter, open approaches may have more than one answer, or at least more than one approach to a solution. Blum and Niss (1991) identified that, to avoid this difficulty, it is tempting to use more closed problems, although this goes against many of the reasons for using problems and open approaches to mathematics:

> 'if assessment and tests are to reflect the spirit, content and complexity inherent in modelling and applications, and are to pay respect to the higher order knowledge and skills they involve, it is necessary to use forms of assessment and testing which cannot be formalized or standardized very easily.'

> (p.65)

This issue of using closed problems was also identified in the previous chapter, where we discussed the idea of traditional word problems as simply 'dressing up' purely mathematical situations. Likewise, Cooper (1994) identified the use of 'contrived' tasks in the assessments we give the children involving problems. Let us look at an example to illustrate this point. Cooper (1994) draws on the following example of a number problem:

This is the sign in a lift at an office block:

> **This lift can carry up to 14 people**

In the morning rush, 269 people want to go up in this lift. How many times does it go up?

Now, how would you solve this problem? Consider the question a moment before continuing with your reading.

Thinking about how we would solve the problem, we would say that if 14 people are getting into the lift each time, then this would be $269 \div 14 = 19$ remainder 3, or the lift would have to make 20 trips because it cannot make a partial trip. And, we would get full marks for this problem according to the marking scheme given for this particular question. Great! So what is wrong with this question? As Cooper points out, although this problem is set in a realistic context, the anticipated approach to the question is wholly unrealistic. For example, are 14 people going to be available to go up in the lift each time? Unlikely. In most work places, people arrive at very different times, even in the morning rush. So sometimes the lift may have 14 people, sometimes 1! If the lift is quite full, people might wait for the next time to go into the lift so sometimes it will be 13 people. So the realistic answer for the above question is that the answer could be anywhere in the range 20 to 269 times! Cooper (1994) goes on to draw conclusions that these types of contrived questions, where the child needs to know what is expected from them in answering the question, rather than it being a genuinely realistic mathematical problem, biases the problem against certain children (for example children with less 'training' in these kinds of questions). Therefore, we can see that these contrived problems may be assessing something more than just problem solving ability – perhaps more like the ability to answer contrived problems. Let us therefore turn our attention to how we might assess children's abilities in solving more genuine mathematical problems.

Critical question

» *Being critical of your own practice, what proportion of problem-solving activities that you use involve genuine problem-solving opportunities? How often are contrived problems unconsciously used?*

Assessing the problem-solving process

Using the SOLO taxonomy

How might we then go about assessing children's abilities in these genuine problems? Looking at the literature on this issue, the answer seems to lie in the processes involved in problem solving and the other open approaches to mathematics. Of course, we have detailed in this book how we see the processes involved in problem solving, and we will return to these shortly. However, different researchers have perceived these processes differently, and we will start by briefly summarising some of their different approaches to assessing problem solving. For example, Collis et al (1986) related problem-solving ability to the SOLO taxonomy, developed by Biggs and Collis (1982, cited in Collis et al, 1986, p.206). The SOLO taxonomy is a way of assessing the level of thinking of children. The levels consist of:

* prestructural level – response shows no relevance;

* unistructural level – only one relevant aspect considered;

* multistructural level – several aspects considered but disjointed;

* relational level – several aspects considered in an integrated whole;

* extended abstract level – where the thinking is taken to another level of abstraction or generalisation.

To exemplify this approach, Collis et al provide the example in Figure 6.1.

Using this context of a number changer or a function machine, they ask different questions related to the SOLO taxonomy levels:

* if 14 is the output, what is the input? (unistructural – dealing with one piece of information);

* if we input 5, what will be the output? (multistructural – dealing with more than one piece of information but still in the order given in the example);

* if the output is 41, what is the input? (relational – need to rearrange the information and show more developed understanding of the reverse process);

* if x is the output and y is the input, how does x relate to y in a formula? (extended abstract – generalising and moving into algebraic expressions).

This is a machine that changes numbers. It adds the number that you put in three times and then adds two more. For example, if you put in a 4, you get out 14.

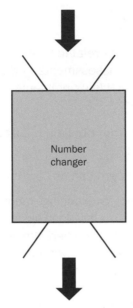

Number changer

Figure 6.1 *A number changer or function machine scenario*

Collis et al therefore used these different contexts for questions at different levels in order to judge what level of thinking primary children and secondary pupils were capable of. The process that they have identified here is the ability to deal with different pieces of information in a more or less connected way. The one possible drawback of this approach is that for the 9 year olds in their study, Collis et al found that they were all at the multistructural level or below, which restricts the applicability of these levels to younger children.

Assessing creativity

Let us continue to examine other possible approaches to assessment. Other researchers have assessed processes that we have directly linked to the problem-solving processes in this book. For example, Haylock (1987) looked at the assessment of creativity in school children. He identified problem-solving tasks where the aim was not necessarily to find the 'correct' answer, but to find as many answers as possible. Adapting one of the questions that he provides:

> *Using the numbers 3, 21, 2, 10, and the symbols +, –, × and ÷, make up as many combinations as you can which equal 17.*

Haylock also identified the idea of 'redefinition' where, given some information, you have to make as many statements using that information as possible. The example he gives is *'write down as many things as you can regarding what the numbers 16 and 36 have in common'*. Here, you are 'redefining' the attributes of the elements of the information you are given. In the same vein, Haylock identified questions involving problem posing, where the aim was, given a particular context (eg some data or information), to come up with as many possible questions as possible. We saw examples of this in the creativity chapter.

Assessing metacognition

Another possible process we can assess related to problem solving is metacognition. Tanner and Jones (2002) used both written assessments and interviews to explore Year 7 and 8 pupils' metacognitive thinking when tackling problems. So, when given a task, the kinds of interview prompts used by them were:

- I am working with you as a partner but I am not as clever as you. Please explain everything that you are doing;

- keep talking to me as much as you can as I am interested in your ideas.

Pupils were assessed against criteria for planning, monitoring, evaluating and reflecting, ie metacognitive thought processes. In terms of written assessments, Tanner and Jones used open tasks such as mathematical modelling tasks, where the open nature of the task meant that the assessment concentrated on the thinking involved rather than the answer. Given a particular mathematical context, they were asked to pose a question regarding the context, then answer the question. Like the interviews, they were asked to detail their planning and their approach to answering the question, alongside how they would present their results. As we can see, in both types of assessments, the emphasis was on externalising the thought processes of pupils.

Using the processes of problem solving

We have given examples of some approaches to the assessment of problem solving based on particular views of the processes involved. However, in this book, we have also taken a particular view of these processes, so let us now describe assessment approaches that are more in line with our view. Firstly, in their study of problem-solving abilities of upper primary children in Australia, Bourke and Stacey (1988) related the questions that they used in a test specifically to the following characteristics of the problem-solving process that they had identified:

- extracting information (understanding the problem and selecting the important information);

- method used in solving the problem (how applicable the method was);

- accuracy in computation;

- correctness of the result;

- quality of explanation of the solution.

In their study, Bourke and Stacey used different items to try and get insight into the different parts of the process, although correctness of the result was applicable to each item. We can see that their problem processes closely match the processes that we identified in Chapter 2. In a slightly different manner, Toh et al (2009) used a 'practical worksheet' to encourage upper secondary and college pupils to externalise the processes that they had identified. Specifically, they looked at the following stages:

- understanding the problem (looking at feelings about the problems, perceived difficulties, and approaches to understanding the problem);

- devising a plan (what are the key concepts, required resources to tackle the problem, writing out the plan);

- carrying out the plan (decisions made during any calculations, details of the mathematical steps);

- checking and extending (show the checking, state how satisfied you are with the problem, state possible adaptations, extensions or generalisations of the problem).

Toh et al used Polya's problem-solving process to provide a framework in which pupils could show in detail all the considerations they were making when tackling a problem. The amount of writing and the type of consideration asked for may not be suitable for primary children. However, it is another way in which we can consider assessing the problem-solving processes.

Szetela (1987) also details a number of different ways in which we can assess the problem-solving process, again largely based around Polya's problem-solving steps. Firstly, they provide the approach of Charles and Lester (1982, cited in Szetela, 1987, p.36). Charles and Lester developed a marking rubric based around the processes of understanding, solving and answering the problem.

- Understanding the problem

  - Completely misinterprets problem (0 marks)

  - Misinterprets part of the problem (1 mark)

  - Understands the problem (2 marks)

- Solving the problem

  - No attempt or inappropriate plan (0 marks)

  - Partially correct plan (1 mark)

  - A plan that could lead to the correct solution (2 marks)

- Answering the problem

  - No answer or wrong answer based on incorrect plan (0 marks)

  - Copying or computational error, or partial answer (1 mark)

  - Correct answer (2 marks)

In Charles and Lester's approach, they identify separate 'dimensions' to the problem-solving process and assess these dimensions accordingly. More simply perhaps, Szetela (1987) also give examples of unidimensional scales for problem solving. For example, this scale from Malone et al (1980, cited by Szetela, 1987, p.37):

- 0 marks – student does not begin problem or his/her work does not make sense;

- 1 mark – student shows some understanding, but reaches a difficulty early on;

- 2 marks – student shows sufficient detail to show that he/she could reach a solution, but is prevented by errors or misinterpretations;

- 3 marks – the problem is very nearly solved except for minor errors;

- 4 marks – an appropriate method is used to reach a valid solution.

We can see that elements of Polya's processes are still included in this scale. Szetela (1987) suggests that Charles and Lester's scale is difficult to apply due to the difficulty of separating out the different dimensions. However, more recent research on assessing problem solving has suggested that a 'multi-dimensional' approach is required to take into account the complexity of open approaches such as problem solving (Jensen, 2007).

Critical question

» *What approaches to assessing problem solving have you seen or used in the classroom? Do solutions to problems tend to be assessed as being right or wrong, or are the processes carried out by children examined?*

Assessment of problem solving in curriculum materials

In addition to drawing on research to guide us in the assessment of problem solving, we can examine curriculum materials which may also exemplify how this assessment process could be carried out. Looking specifically at materials from England and Wales, as we write this book, schools and teachers are preparing themselves to deliver a new curriculum from September 2014. Included in the aims of this new national curriculum for mathematics is that children can reason mathematically and solve problems by applying their mathematical knowledge (Department for Education, 2013). However, within the new programme of study, what children are expected to achieve in relation to problem solving is included within particular areas of mathematics such as number, measurement, geometry etc. Therefore, it is difficult to extract the requirements for problem solving more generally to help us guide our assessments. In addition, one of the difficulties that schools will face with regards to assessment within the new curriculum is the abolishing of the use of attainment levels in reporting on child progress. However, we can examine the out-going national curriculum, which did provide attainment targets related to 'using and applying' mathematics across the different areas of mathematics to be taught (DfES and QCA 1999, pp 87–88).

> *Teachers should expect attainment at a given level in this attainment target to be demonstrated through activities in which the mathematics from the other attainment targets is at, or very close to, the same level.*
>
> *Level 1*
>
> *Pupils use mathematics as an integral part of classroom activities. They represent their work with objects or pictures and discuss it. They recognise and use a simple pattern or relationship.*

Level 2

Pupils select the mathematics they use in some classroom activities. They discuss their work using mathematical language and are beginning to represent it using symbols and simple diagrams. They explain why an answer is correct.

Level 3

Pupils try different approaches and find ways of overcoming difficulties that arise when they are solving problems. They are beginning to organise their work and check results. Pupils discuss their mathematical work and are beginning to explain their thinking. They use and interpret mathematical symbols and diagrams. Pupils show that they understand a general statement by finding particular examples that match it.

Level 4

Pupils are developing their own strategies for solving problems and are using these strategies both in working within mathematics and in applying mathematics to practical contexts. They present information and results in a clear and organised way. They search for a solution by trying out ideas of their own.

Level 5

In order to carry through tasks and solve mathematical problems, pupils identify and obtain necessary information. They check their results, considering whether these are sensible. Pupils show understanding of situations by describing them mathematically using symbols, words and diagrams. They draw simple conclusions of their own and give an explanation of their reasoning.

Level 6

Pupils carry through substantial tasks and solve quite complex problems by independently breaking them down into smaller, more manageable tasks. They interpret, discuss and synthesise information presented in a variety of mathematical forms. Pupils' writing explains and informs their use of diagrams. Pupils are beginning to give mathematical justifications.

Level 7

Starting from problems or contexts that have been presented to them, pupils progressively refine or extend the mathematics used to generate fuller solutions. They give a reason for their choice of mathematical presentation, explaining features they have selected. Pupils justify their generalisations, arguments or solutions, showing some insight into the mathematical structure of the problem. They appreciate the difference between mathematical explanation and experimental evidence.

Level 8

Pupils develop and follow alternative approaches. They reflect on their own lines of enquiry when exploring mathematical tasks; in doing so they introduce and use a range of mathematical techniques. Pupils convey mathematical or statistical meaning through precise and consistent use of symbols that is sustained throughout the work. They examine generalisations or solutions reached in an activity, commenting constructively on the reasoning and logic or the process employed, or the results obtained, and make further progress in the activity as a result.

Exceptional performance

Pupils give reasons for the choices they make when investigating within mathematics itself or when using mathematics to analyse tasks; these reasons explain why particular lines of enquiry or procedures are followed and others rejected. Pupils apply the mathematics they know in familiar and unfamiliar contexts. Pupils use mathematical language and symbols effectively in presenting a convincing reasoned argument. Their reports include mathematical justifications, explaining their solutions to problems involving a number of features or variables.

Reformulating attainment levels by processes

Looking at the different attainment levels, and guided by our previous discussion, which looked at different dimensions within the problem-solving processes, we can try and identify and organise different dimensions within the attainment levels. In fact, we have categorised the identified dimensions as 'understanding and solving', 'representing', 'thinking and reasoning', and 'checking and metacognition', echoing much of our discussion in the previous chapters. In each case, we have indicated what level each statement corresponds to although we have inserted some statements in italics if these seemed to be missing from the original attainment levels.

Understanding and solving

- Using mathematics in problem situations (1).

- Selecting mathematics for problem situations (2).

- Trying different approaches to overcome difficulties (3).

- Developing their own strategies and applying these in real contexts (4).

- Identifying necessary information for solving problems (5).

- Breaking down problems into more manageable forms and interpreting and synthesising a variety of information formats (6).

- Refining and extending problems to generate fuller solutions (7).

- Developing alternative approaches to solutions (8).

- Applying mathematics to unfamiliar situations (Exceptional).

In this dimension of understanding and solving, we can see the progression in terms of how children are required to use more complex solution approaches, to understand the problems in real-life situations, and to break down problems and extract the relevant information in these more complex problem situations. It also includes, latterly, developing alternative solution strategies and extending problems through problem posing.

Representing

- Representing their work with objects or pictures, and able to discuss it (1).

- Representing their work with symbols and simple diagrams, and able to use mathematical language to discuss it (2).

- Using and interpreting symbols and diagrams (3).

- *Beginning to use writing alongside symbols and diagrams (4).*

- Using symbols, writing and diagrams (5).

- Using writing to inform and explain the use of diagrams (6).

- Explaining their choice of representations (7).

- Conveying meaning through precise and consistent use of symbols (8).

- Using mathematical language and symbols to present a convincing, reasoned argument (Exceptional).

In their development of representing problems, as part of the problem-solving process, children begin with simple objects and pictures, progress to being able to discuss the problem (ie represent it through spoken words), then onto the use of the written word. Latterly, they begin to explain their use of representations for the problems, and then use mathematical language and symbols in a clear precise way.

Thinking and reasoning

- Recognising a simple pattern or relationship (1).

- Explaining why an answer is correct (2).

- Explaining their thinking, showing why a general statement may be true through the use of particular examples (3).

- *Beginning to draw reasoned conclusions (4).*

- Drawing conclusions and explaining their reasoning (5).

- Beginning to provide mathematical explanations (6).

- Justifying any generalisations, arguments or solutions, and having mathematical insight of the problem (7).

- Examining the logic behind any generalisations, arguments or solutions of a problem and constructively developing these (8).

- Justifying and explaining approaches in investigations or problems involving a number of features or variables (Exceptional).

In progressing in their thinking or reasoning, children begin by recognising simple patterns, then move on to explaining their thinking, firstly using particular examples to justify generalisations, then drawing out conclusions from the information provided. Latterly, they use more mathematical ways of thinking, and justify their mathematical thinking, examining the logic behind it. This is extended to justifying their thinking over a number of variables associated with a problem.

Checking and metacognition

- Beginning to organise their work and check results (3).

- Organising information and their work (4).

- Checking whether their results are sensible (5).

- *Beginning to use mathematical explanations to check results as well as experimental approaches* (6).

- Appreciating the difference between a mathematical explanation and experimental evidence (7).

- Reflecting on their lines of enquiry (8).

- Explaining why certain lines of enquiry are followed or rejected (Exceptional).

With this final identified dimension, the initial levels are missing since, as we suggested in the metacognition section in the thinking chapter, younger children are unlikely to be able to examine their thinking. When they do start to examine their thinking, they begin by organising their work and checking their results. This checking then extends to more mathematical explanations of why a result might be correct, rather than looking at whether individual cases are correct for a problem. Latterly, they can look more broadly at how they approached a problem and whether other approaches to a problem may have been better or worse.

In using the 1999 national curriculum attainment levels for 'using and applying', alongside our previous considerations of the problem process, and also the different approaches to assessment including the issue of multiple dimensions, we feel that the rearranged attainment levels provide a reasonable, detailed list of possible assessment criteria, which also draw out the different processes within problem solving and other open approaches. These levels are also able to provide some indication of what we might expect from children in carrying out problem-solving activities. It is expected that the majority of children at the end of primary school will achieve a level 4. This would look like the following, according to the above discussion.

Level 4 children

- Develop their own strategies and apply these in real contexts;

- Begin to use writing alongside symbols and diagrams;

- Begin to draw reasoned conclusions;

- Organise information and their work.

For high-attaining primary children, perhaps achieving level 6 at the end of primary school, their problem-solving abilities would look like this:

Level 6 children

• Break down problems into more manageable forms and interpret and synthesise a variety of information formats;

• Use writing to inform and explain the use of diagrams;

• Begin to provide mathematical justifications;

• Begin to use mathematical explanations to check results as well as experimental approaches.

Critical questions

» Given the above possible ways of assessing mathematical problem solving by children, which approach if any would you choose? Why?

» What constraints might you experience in trying to implement any of the possible approaches to assessment?

Further considerations from the classroom

So perhaps it is time to reflect upon how you currently assess problem solving in your school. What assessment strategies do you use and which are currently used in your school? Once you have identified these, reflect critically and try to determine why they are used and how they support accurate assessment. For example, do you see 'thumbs up' at the end of an activity or at the end of a lesson? Why is this strategy used? Is it perhaps because other teachers are known to use it and it has just been absorbed into practice? How does it support accurate assessment? You may well come to the conclusion that it doesn't actually identify or support anything! Quite often lower ability children will over-assess their ability and higher ability children will underestimate theirs. But, even if children were capable of understanding and of grading their own understanding accurately and indicating that with their thumbs, how does the teacher remember and/or record children's responses? What is the value of an assessment technique where the teacher has no idea which of their class of 30 had their thumbs up, down or wavering horizontally as soon as their hands are put down? As it is impossible to remember exactly, and therefore to use the information to inform future planning or intervention, 'thumbs up', as a strategy for assessment, can quite quickly be identified as a complete waste of time.

While reflecting upon your own assessment strategies, you must also consider the range of problems children have had the opportunity to explore. The types of problems you present to children, and when and how you present these problems, will influence what you are able to assess. For example, the following problem posed as an independent activity on Friday after a week of practising addition will inform your short-term assessment, allowing you to assess whether children can add:

David had 25 books. Patrick gave him another 37 books. How many books does David have altogether?

The following problem, on the other hand, posed as a paired activity will allow you to assess whether children can calculate and solve problems:

You have two jugs. One holds 4 litres and the other holds 9 litres when full, but neither have any markings on them. You also have a bucket of water. How can you measure 6 litres of water?

Neither the immediate prior learning nor the language used in the second problem indicates a route to finding a solution (and there is more than one solution). We can begin to use one of the above methods of assessment, for example the scale mentioned earlier from Malone et al (1980, cited by Szetela, 1987, p.37), to judge children's competence in solving problems. But the fact that this is presented as a paired activity will also give us an opportunity to listen to children's ideas, reasoning and justifications and to further assess their problem-solving skills. The second problem could also have been presented as a group activity using the roles discussed in Chapter 4, and still allowing the teacher to listen to discussion and make assessments.

There are times, however, when you may wish to assess children's proficiency in a particular skill, and presenting a mathematical question in context is a good way to do this. Therefore, you need to decide the purpose of presenting a problem at the planning stage – is it to assess mathematical proficiency or to practise problem-solving skills? This must also be kept in mind when marking work. What are you assessing:

•   the maths within the problem?

or

•   children's ability to solve problems?

As stated earlier, problem solving is embedded into mathematical topic areas in the national curriculum (DfE, 2013), and the danger is that teachers teach and assess the maths content rather than the problem-solving aspects of it. The end of Key Stage 2 SAT tests are also changing in line with the new curriculum and these reflect the current government's view that problem solving is at the heart of understanding mathematics. The old paper B (calculator) is to be replaced with paper 2, focussing on problem solving. This may result in problem solving earning a higher status in schools in order to ensure children achieve well in reported assessment tests. Though standardised tests and the publication of school results are not necessarily conducive to good teaching, the 'knock on' effect for the teaching of problem solving may well be.

It has also been proposed recently that, in order to fully bring SATs into line with the new curriculum, the compulsory national curriculum test will, from 2016, cover Attainment Levels 3 to 6 instead of Levels 3 to 5, and mental mathematics will no longer be part of the formal assessment. If this is the case, we would urge schools not to lose focus on the importance of learning and using mental strategies. Without these strategies and skills, children will have difficulty in all areas of calculation, which will impact on the knowledge they bring to problem solving and to their confidence in and attitude to maths generally.

Critical questions

» *What whole-school approaches to assessing problem-solving skills have you experienced? To what extent would you say that these approaches are focussing on problem-solving skills?*

» *How might you start to incorporate some of the assessment methods discussed in this chapter into your own practice?*

Critical reflections

In this chapter, we began by discussing the difficulties faced in assessing children's approaches to problem solving, whether these are issues related to teacher knowledge, as highlighted by Ofsted, or simply related to the more open-ended nature of problem solving as highlighted by Sangster (2012) and Blum and Niss (1991). And in fact, in examining even more open-ended approaches to mathematics in the next chapter, we are going to face these difficulties to a greater extent. One of the conclusions that we initially drew in this chapter was that, if we are indeed looking at problem solving as a more open approach to mathematics, then the closed questions that we tend to use in the classroom or in child assessments are not going to effectively capture the skills that children might bring to the problem.

In highlighting these difficulties then, the approaches that we have suggested, based on suggestions from the literature, are related to actual problem-solving processes that have been identified by researchers. Now, in some cases, these processes may be quite different to processes we have highlighted in this book, and that simply comes down to the way that different researchers have tried to make sense of the problem-solving process. What we emphasise here is that, rather than focussing on the answer to the problem (we saw earlier that getting the right answer is only one small part of the problem-solving process) it is much better to evaluate the broader processes involved. As it happens, we feel that the problem-solving processes that we have put forward match pretty well the old national curriculum guidance materials for assessing problem solving from the Department for Education and Employment, and Qualifications and Curriculum Authority (1999). Therefore, as we move over to a new curriculum, let us not lose these useful approaches to assessment. Rather, let us see how we can use these guidance materials, or our interpretation of this guidance, under the process headings of Understanding and solving, Representing, Thinking and reasoning, and Checking and metacognition, and see how we can effectively implement these approaches in the classroom. In doing so, at least we can be clear as to why we are using such approaches.

Taking it further

In identifying the problematic nature of some of the questions that we use in assessing children's approaches to problem solving, the work of our colleague here at Durham University, Barry Cooper, has been very influential. Therefore, we recommend that you read the journal paper highlighted earlier in the chapter, or Barry Cooper and Máiréad Dunne's book on the topic.

In terms of relating problem-solving processes to assessment, although the reference is rather old, a clear outline to different approaches to assessment is provided by Szetela (1987). More recently, the paper by Tanner and Jones (2002) provides a clear, interesting read focussing specifically on metacognition.

Cooper, B (1994) Authentic testing in mathematics? The boundary between everyday and mathematical knowledge in national curriculum testing in English schools. *Assessment in Education: Principles, Policy & Practice*, 1(2), 143–166

Cooper, B, & Dunne, M (1999) *Assessing children's mathematical knowledge: social class, sex, and problem-solving*. Buckingham: Open University Press

Szetela, W (1987) The problem of evaluation in problem solving: can we find solutions? *The Arithmetic Teacher*, November, 36–41

Tanner, H, & Jones, S (2002) Assessing children's mathematical thinking in practical modelling situations. *Teaching Mathematics and its Applications*, 21(4), 145–159

7 Open approaches to mathematics

Key issues in this chapter

- This chapter extends your thinking and applies the ideas developed, through considering the processes involved in problem solving, to other 'open approaches' to mathematics.

- In addition to defining 'open approaches' to mathematics, it looks at the specific examples of investigations, mathematical modelling, and the realistic mathematics education approach.

- In looking at these different open approaches, it demonstrates that all these approaches are underpinned by the same problem-solving processes highlighted in the book so far.

- Having established this connection, it relates it to how you can 'open out' your teaching of the subject in the classroom.

Introduction

Previous chapters have taken a detailed look at the processes involved in problem solving, relating the ideas to creativity and mathematical thinking. They have provided a clear outline of what is involved in problem solving, and just why it is such an important part of learning and doing mathematics. However, focussing specifically on problem solving has in some ways narrowed the discussion. This chapter and the next broaden the discussion to show that these important processes apply to other areas of mathematical activity. The use of *investigations* in the classroom and also *mathematical modelling* are examined, both of which are closely related to problem-solving activities. Also, although this has been touched upon already, the chapter returns to the ideas of *problem posing* as a broader way of incorporating important processes into the teaching and learning of mathematics. Developing these ideas further, these processes are examined in the context of theoretically-based approaches such as *realistic mathematics education,* providing further insight into why such approaches should be adopted in the classroom. This then provides the basis for discussing, in the next chapter, the enrichment of teaching and the engagement of children. We begin by looking at investigations within mathematics.

Investigations

Chapter 2 carefully defined what we meant by problem solving. The definition that we arrived at was that a problem is a problem if the route to its solution is not obvious (Jones, 2003). In general, a problem has a clear solution. When we consider investigations, however, they do not necessarily have such a clear solution. Ponte (2007) provides the following definition for investigations:

> *Mathematical investigations share common aspects with other kinds of problem solving activities. They involve complex thinking processes and require a high involvement and a creative stand from the student. However, they also involve some distinctive features. While mathematical problems tend to be characterized by well-defined givens and goals, investigations are much looser in that respect.*
>
> (Ponte, 2007, p.420)

What distinguishes investigations from problems is that the end-points for the mathematical activity are less constrained. Let us look at an example to illustrate this point. This is an investigation from the NRICH website developed by the University of Cambridge (http://nrich. maths.org). The investigation involves examining combinations of four consecutive numbers. For example, let us start off with 1, 2, 3 and 4. Using the consecutive numbers chosen, we investigate what happens if we use different combinations of + and – on these numbers. We might begin in the following way:

$$1+2+3+4=10$$
$$1-2+3+4=6$$
$$1+2-3+4=4$$
$$1+2+3-4=2$$
$$1-2-3+4=0$$
$$1-2+3-4=-2$$
$$1+2-3-4=-4$$
$$1-2-3-4=-8$$

Already, looking at these calculations, they raise a number of questions. Firstly, are we sure that we have got all the possible combinations of the four numbers? Secondly, why are all the answers even numbers? Is there a good reason for that? Thirdly, why is there no calculation that gives us – 6? Is this related to the fact that we only ever have a positive 1 at the beginning of the calculation? Would it make a difference if we allowed a + or – to be in front of the first number? Fourthly, what happens if we change the consecutive numbers, say to 2, 3, 4 and 5? Or what happens if we just have three, or even two consecutive numbers? As we can see, this simple task which is suitable for primary children is amazingly rich in terms of the mathematical opportunities it provides. One reason for this is the open nature of the investigation, which means that the solution of the problem is not constrained. That is a key distinguishing feature of investigations compared to problems.

The important role of problem posing in investigations

In terms of the processes involved in carrying out investigations, are there any differences between investigations and the processes outlined for problem solving? Ponte (2001) highlights the following processes as being involved in investigations:

*   searching for patterns;

*   formulating questions;

*   testing ideas and assumptions;

*   justifying ideas and proving conjectures;

*   reflecting on your thinking/reasoning;

*   generalising.

Many of the processes identified by Ponte are the same as those we identified for problem solving. However, there is one key difference which Ponte (2001) emphasises. By definition, investigations are more open-ended than problems, therefore much of the initial work that is done in an investigation is clarifying the questions to be asked and the context and conditions in which the investigation takes place. An essential part of an investigation is the formulating or posing of problems. In problem solving, initially at least, the question to be tackled is much clearer. However, in investigations we need a process of clarification which is provided by the process of problem posing. In the previous chapter on creativity, we identified problem posing as a key part of creative thinking. Likewise, Ponte (2007) highlights the opportunities for creative thinking provided by investigations as well as by problem solving. Let us look at one more example of an investigation to illustrate the creative thinking and problem posing involved. Again, we turn to Ponte (2001) for the following example:

> *Consider triangles with integer sides. There are 3 sides with perimeter 12 units. Investigate.*

The first step we need to take, as we highlighted above, is to clarify the question that we need to answer. We know the context of the investigation (we are looking at triangles) but we need to pose our own problems to give us a start. So, let us ask whether we can draw such a triangle as described above (Figure 7.1).

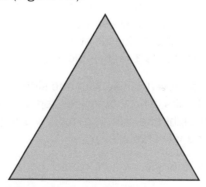

Figure 7.1 *Triangle with each side 4 units in length*

Let us see whether we can draw another triangle that meets the conditions (Figure 7.2).

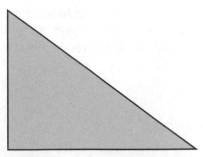

Figure 7.2 *Triangle with sides 3, 4 and 5 units in length*

The next question we might ask is whether there are combinations of unit lengths that cannot form a triangle. Let us try the extreme combination of sides 1 unit, 1 unit and 10 units (Figure 7.3).

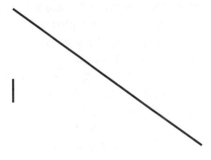

Figure 7.3 *Sides of 1, 1 and 10 units in length*

We see that this combination cannot form a triangle. We can ask the additional question of why it cannot. The reason seems to be that the two smallest sides, if laid end to end, still only total 2 units, so we cannot have a third side of 10 units. So a condition seems to be that in an arrangement of sides, the longest side must be shorter than the other two sides added together. The next question we may ask is, bearing the previous condition in mind, can we have a triangle where one of the sides is still 1 unit in length? Let us list the possible combinations where one of the sides is 1 unit (Table 7.1).

It seems that it is not possible to have triangle with one side 1 unit long. Even when we have the combination of 1, 5 and 6 units, where two sides together equal the length of the third side, which results in just a straight line, not a triangle. Moving on, if the smallest side is 2 units, do we have a possible triangle (Table 7.2)?

We do appear to have one triangle, which would be a very thin isosceles triangle (Figure 7.4).

Table 7.1 *Possible combinations with one side 1 unit long*

Side 1	Side 2	Side 3	Possible?
1	2	9	✗
1	3	8	✗
1	4	7	✗
1	5	6	✗

Table 7.2 *Possible combinations with one side 2 units long*

Side 1	Side 2	Side 3	Possible?
2	2	8	✗
2	3	7	✗
2	4	6	✗
2	5	5	✓

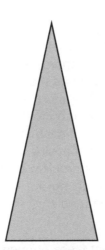

Figure 7.4 *Triangle with sides 2, 5 and 5 units in length*

If we have one side 3 units long, the only combinations we can have (discarding those involving sides with 1 or 2 units, which we have already considered) are 3, 3 and 6; and 3, 4 and 5. The first is not a possible triangle, and we have already identified the second in the right-angled triangle. Finally, for a triangle with one side 4 units long, discarding combinations involving

1, 2 and 3 unit sides, the only possibility is the 4, 4 and 4 combination – the equilateral triangle. So we can answer one last question – is it true that there are only three possible triangles? Indeed, this seems to be the case.

In the above example, we can see that this simple mathematical context again provides a rich opportunity for children to explore triangles. It is clear that problem posing plays a vital part in the investigation process. Linking back to the idea of creativity, we emphasised that creativity involved both connecting to new areas or questions, and also reflecting upon the usefulness of the connection or question. Therefore, we could reflect, either at the end of a particular cycle of investigative activity, or during a given cycle, on whether the questions we are asking are the most useful, or whether we could be asking better or simply different questions, which would lead to the exploration of different ideas or make our thinking more concise. As we highlighted previously, we could metacognitively monitor our mathematical thinking, and problematise our thinking during the investigation.

Critical questions

» *In your experience, how often are more open investigative activities used in the classroom? What constraints do teachers face in implementing such approaches?*

» *If you have used or seen such approaches in the classroom, what is the impact on children both in terms of their development of understanding, and also their engagement?*

Open approaches to mathematics

Before we move on and look at mathematical modelling as another form of mathematical activity that we can use in the classroom, let us take a step back, and briefly discuss in more general terms the notion of 'open approaches' to the teaching of mathematics. We saw in the previous section on investigations that one way we might differentiate between investigations and problem solving is the more open nature of investigations. This open characteristic in turn encourages children to problem pose as part of making sense of the task. However, we need to sound a note of caution here. We highlighted in earlier chapters that the posing of problems and problematising our thinking is an important part of the problem-solving process. Therefore, this problem posing is not restricted to investigations. We can apply the same processes when we are tackling problems, by 'opening out' the problems, that is by looking for related problems, in order to develop our understanding of the problem context further.

In order to make sense of the different types of open approaches to mathematics, we can turn to the literature to see how researchers have dealt with this. Pehkonen (1997) describes the use of 'open-ended' problems in the classroom, which includes investigations and also realistic mathematical approaches which we will come to later. Silver (1994) also talks about problem posing as an approach, which we discussed previously. He uses the term *inquiry-based approaches* to talk about these open approaches to mathematics, and includes *ill-structured* problems and the application of mathematics to such problems as another

Table 7.3 Classification of 'open approaches' to mathematics

Starting situation	Goal situation	
	CLOSED (ie exactly explained)	OPEN
CLOSED (ie exactly explained)	Closed problems	Open-ended problems; real-life investigations; problem fields; problem variations ('what-if' method);
OPEN	Real-life problems; Problem variations ('what-if' method)	Real-life situations; problem variations ('what-if' method); projects; problem posing

approach – we will also discuss the latter in the next section on mathematical modelling. More generally, Lee et al (2003, p.165) provides the above overview for characterising different open approaches to mathematics (Table 7.3).

We see that we have problems and investigations in real-life contexts, and we will discuss these more in mathematical modelling. Problem variations are described by Lee et al (2003) as situations where we are asking 'what-if'. Problem fields are described as sequences of problems. We would tend to categorise both of these under problem posing more generally, as we have seen in previous examples where the posing of questions such as 'what-if' has led to a string of problems being tackled. Lee et al also include projects which are extended pieces of work. Silver (1994) gives the example of children writing 'books' to describe particular mathematical concepts to other children. Perhaps projects do stand apart from the other open approaches, but we emphasise that the other approaches, whatever we might call them, share many common characteristics in terms of the thinking processes that they draw upon from children. They differ mainly in the nature of the starting or goal situations. We would suggest that it is these processes that are important, and which we need to keep in mind in providing learning experiences for children, rather than the specifics of which open approach we would use, since we can encourage children to 'open up' their mathematical thinking in whatever context.

Mathematical modelling

In Lee et al's (2003) characterisation of different 'open' mathematical activities, the suggestion of 'real-life' activities strongly came through. In this section, we will look more closely at these, although we call them 'mathematical modelling' activities for reasons which will soon become clear. Of course, as we emphasised in the previous section, there are strong links between these activities and the problem-solving activities that we have previously discussed. Indeed, Lesh (1981) initially referred to mathematical modelling activities as 'applied mathematical problem solving', specifically involving 'real' problems or 'realistic' situations. Likewise, Blum and Niss (1991) highlight that mathematical modelling activities begin with a 'real' problem which, through a process of simplification and restructuring, results in a 'model' of the realistic situation. In developing this model and representing the real world situation in terms of mathematics, Blum and Niss refer to this as the *mathematisation* of the real world situation. Lesh and Doerr (2003) alternatively refer to these activities as 'model-elicting' activities, because children are asked to develop a model of the real world situation. They contrast this with the use of traditional word problems (see Figure 7.5).

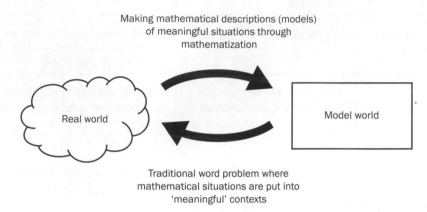

Making mathematical descriptions (models)
of meaningful situations through
mathematization

Real world

Model world

Traditional word problem where
mathematical situations are put into
'meaningful' contexts

Figure 7.5 *Contrast between mathematical modelling and traditional word problems (from Lesh and Doerr, 2003)*

What we are usually doing with traditional problems, particularly word problems, is that we know what mathematical concepts they contain and what operations we want children to apply to these problems. The problem is used to provide a 'real world' context for the mathematics, perhaps to make the problem more meaningful to children. But we have to be careful what we mean here by 'real world'. Real how? Traditional word problems do not originate from authentic contexts but are fashioned for the purposes of the mathematics. In model-eliciting or mathematical modelling activities however, mathematisation of the contexts are carried out in a way that is meaningful to the children (English and Watters, 2005; Redmond et al, 2012). In fact Lesh (1981) identifies the attributes of 'real' problems as being meaningful and interesting to children. Blum and Niss (1991, p.40), on the other hand, describe traditional word problems as simply 'dressing up' purely mathematical situations and providing a 'distorted picture of reality'.

Examples of mathematical modelling activities

Let us provide an example of a mathematical modelling activity to illustrate these identified characteristics. Purdue University in the United States has a number of examples of possible modelling activities, suitable mainly for secondary pupils but some for primary children as well (see https://engineering.purdue.edu/ENE/Research /SGMM/CASESTUDIESKIDSWEB/ index.htm, accessed 3rd January 2014). One is an example of a 'historic hotel'. The Purdue website provides far more details but the essence of the problem is as follows.

> *Your mother inherits a historic hotel and asks your advice on managing the hotel. The hotel has 60 rooms, and the previous owner stated that all the rooms tended to be occupied if he set the room rate at £45 per night. However, when*

he increased the tariff, for every £2 increase, one less room would be occupied. With regards to cleaning and maintaining the rooms, they tended to cost £3 per day if the room was occupied. How much should your mother charge per night to maximise profits?

This problem may be more suitable for upper primary children. Also, it is a good opportunity for children to use spreadsheets to solve the problem. If the charge is £45 per night per room, with 60 rooms, income per night would be 60 × £45 = £2700. However, there would be cleaning and maintenance costs of 60 × £3 = £180. Therefore, the profit per night would be £2700 – £180 = £2520. We can use a spreadsheet to see how all the different values change when we increase the cost of the room (Figure 7.6). Children can use the spreadsheet to calculate the different values, rather than calculating everything themselves. It therefore allows children to focus on the modelling processes and the mathematics concepts, rather than repetitive calculations.

	A	B	C	D	E
1	Charge per room	Occupancy	Income (Charge per room * Occupancy)	Total maintenance costs (3* occupancy)	Profit (Income - total maintenance)
2	45	60	2700	180	2520
3	47	59	2773	177	2596
4	49	58	2842	174	2668
5	51	57	2907	171	2736
6	53	56	2968	168	2800
7	55	55	3025	165	2860
8	57	54	3078	162	2916
9	59	53	3127	159	2968
10	61	52	3172	156	3016
11	63	51	3213	153	3060
12	65	50	3250	150	3100
13	67	49	3283	147	3136
14	69	48	3312	144	3168
15	71	47	3337	141	3196
16	73	46	3358	138	3220
17	75	45	3375	135	3240
18	77	44	3388	132	3256
19	79	43	3397	129	3268
20	81	42	3402	126	3276
21	83	41	3403	123	3280
22	85	40	3400	120	3280
23	87	39	3393	117	3276
24	89	38	3382	114	3268

Figure 7.6 *Output from spreadsheet*

We can see that the maximum profit is achieved at between £83 and £85, therefore we could suggest a charge of £84 per night. The important point in the above example is the illustration of having to develop a 'model' of the real world situation provided. And we can see that the model is not a translation to some simple mathematical operation that we might experience in traditional word problems. But we can tackle the complexities of the activity using ICT.

Important processes in mathematical modelling

Having examined an example of a mathematical modelling activity and what might be involved in such an activity, let us examine more closely the types of processes involved in mathematical modelling. In looking at the solving of real problems, Lesh (1981) highlighted the following processes:

*   simplifying the original situation;

*   creating a mapping between the real and model situations;

*   investigating the properties of the model to make further predictions;

*   translating the predictions from the model back to the original situation.

Alternatively, English and Watters (2005) highlight that modelling activities provide opportunities for children to construct models and represent situations, predict and conjecture using their models, and explain and justify their thinking. When we look at these processes, once again, we see strong parallels with the processes highlighted for problem solving and for investigations. The way we would view these processes would be that, initially, we try and represent the real world situation in some way and then reason with the representation (model) to see what conclusions we can draw. All the time, we would be reflecting on the adequacy of the representation used and our reasoning. Therefore, once again, we see mathematical modelling as part of the wider, more open approaches to mathematics. In the case of mathematical modelling, what differentiates these activities from others is that, as Lesh (1981) puts it, the situations involves more 'noise', with more characteristics that are possibly irrelevant which we need to discount when developing the models of the situations.

Benefits of modelling activities

Having seen the links between these modelling activities and the open approaches to mathematics, what might be the rationale for using modelling activities in our classrooms? Blum and Niss (1991) provide a number of arguments. Firstly, undertaking mathematical modelling activities can be used to develop both mathematical skills and understanding in children. Secondly, in terms of interest and attitudes as well as understanding, Lesh (1981) and Boaler (2001) highlight that modelling activities develop the interest of children in mathematics. We will explore in the next chapter why such activities are more 'engaging' for children. However, Lesh (1981) emphasises that children involved in solving more personally meaningful problems, and having the opportunity to bring their own thinking to the problems, are creatively more engaged in the activity. The third rationale provided by Blum and Niss is that the competencies developed through such activities equip children as citizens in the future. Related to this, Blum and Niss also argue that the mathematics children learn needs to be useful to them. The final argument they provide is that, in our teaching, we need to provide a more comprehensive picture of what doing mathematics is all about, and these activities provide just that. In addition to these benefits, we can also link to two other obvious benefits, one of which we have already highlighted. Modelling activities provide good opportunities to incorporate the use of ICT in the teaching and learning of the subject. Lesh (1981) emphasises the use of calculators in such activities so that the focus is on the more challenging aspects of tackling the real problem. Likewise, we emphasised the use of spreadsheets previously. Secondly, Lesh also highlights the use of other people as a resource for tackling real problems. This links back to the highlighting of discussion as facilitating the problem-solving process.

Drawbacks of modelling activities

Although we have highlighted some of the benefits of modelling activities (which largely overlap with the benefits of more open approaches to mathematics), there are some drawbacks identified as well. Blum and Niss (1991) identify, among other things, teachers' concerns over the time taken for such activities. Secondly, teachers see these activities as being too difficult for children, ie the non-routine problem-solving processes are more difficult than the simple carrying out of operations. Thirdly, modelling activities can place greater demands on the teachers themselves, in terms of the subject knowledge required and maintaining 'control' over the activities of children. These are all possible drawbacks that are echoed in the problem-solving literature more generally, and we would argue that, to tackle these drawbacks, we need teachers to see the importance of such open activities in mathematics and to develop a clearer idea of what is involved in such activities.

One other criticism, raised by Blum and Niss (1991), is the availability of such activities, especially for primary children. Indeed, if we examine such resources as the NRICH website, most possible modelling activities are for secondary pupils, particularly upper secondary. But let us try and identify a few other examples. Lesh and Doerr (2003) provide three different possible examples that could be used with primary children, all of which are provided on the Purdue University website. One is the Big Foot problem. The resources provided include pictures of footprints of different animals, and also a picture of a footprint possibly belonging to Big Foot. The activity is for children to try and estimate the height of Big Foot from this information. The second activity is the Volleyball problem, which involves children being given different data on a group of Volleyball players (eg height, height they can jump, speed of running, serve and spike results), and they need to come up with a system for ranking these players. The third activity involves paper airplanes. The Purdue website provides sample data from a competition, or children can be asked to make their own planes. Then they are asked to fly their planes around different courses (straight, round a corner, and an inverted U-shape) and to record data on total distance, distance from target, and time in flight. Children are asked to decide on designs for best 'floaters' (time in air), most accurate, best boomerang and best overall planes. English and Watters (2005) also detail the paper airplane problem, providing specific resources for working with primary children. We encourage teachers to explore all these and other activities on the Purdue website. We would emphasise the importance of taking the activities and adapting them according to the needs of children that you work with, while maintaining the essence of what is important in mathematical modelling.

A further example

Let us examine one further example from research, this time in a little more detail. English and Watters (2005) suggest the Beans problem, specifically for primary children. They provide some contextual information to make the problem more meaningful for children (for example, relating the activity to themes covered recently in the classroom in other subjects such as science), then they provide the following data to the children (Table 7.4).

Table 7.4 Bean plant activity

	Sunlight				Shade		
Bean plants	Week 6	Week 8	Week 10	Bean plants	Week 6	Week 8	Week 10
Row 1	8	12	13	Row 1	5	9	15
Row 2	9	11	14	Row 2	5	8	14
Row 3	9	14	18	Row 3	6	9	12
Row 4	10	11	17	Row 4	6	10	13

The specific context of the above data was that a local farmer had being growing beans under different conditions, planted in rows, and measuring the yield of beans after 6, 8 and 10 weeks. The children were asked to make a recommendation of which was the best condition for growing beans, and to predict the weight of the beans under each condition after 12 weeks. Children may model the situations in the following ways. Firstly, they might find the mean weight at each point in time, averaging over the different rows of beans (Table 7.5).

Table 7.5 Bean plant activity – averages

	Sunlight				Shade		
Bean plants	Week 6	Week 8	Week 10	Bean plants	Week 6	Week 8	Week 10
Average	9.0	12.0	15.5	Row 1	5.5	9.0	13.5

Children might then plot graphs to show the pattern of data in each condition (Figure 7.7).

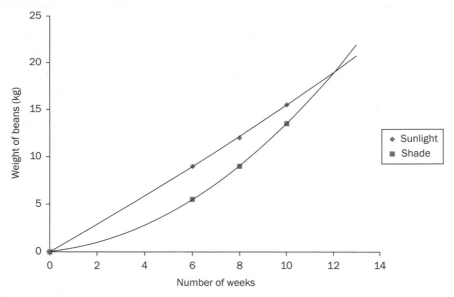

Figure 7.7 *Plotting the bean plant data*

In the above example, we have included a few additional details. We assumed that the weight of beans at week 0 was 0 kg in both cases. Then we fitted a curve to both and found that the conditions gave the same amount of weight at week 12 (around 19 kg), but then the shaded condition overtakes the sunlight condition. So we would probably recommend the latter. But this is dependent on the way we have modelled the situation, and the assumptions we have made. We would have to go back and reflect on these decisions to see whether we could have modelled the situation more accurately. Once again, we hope that the problem-solving skills, and particularly the mathematical thinking skills that can emerge from the problem, are made clear.

Critical questions

» *Have you ever used or experienced mathematical modelling activities in the classroom? If so, what impact did they have? If not, why do you think this is the case?*

» *One of the potential difficulties, in terms of incorporating mathematical modelling in the classroom, is the availability of suitable activities. Can you come up with any contexts or activities that could be developed into mathematical modelling opportunities?*

Realistic mathematics education

In the last section, we highlighted the importance of trying to use authentic problem-solving tasks with children, rather than simply 'dressing up' (Blum and Niss, 1991) tasks in what we think may be a realistic context, but which may not be realistic for the children. This problem has been noted elsewhere, for example by Verschaffel, De Corte and Lasure (1994) who identified what they termed *'an alarmingly small number of realistic responses or additional comments based on realistic considerations'*(p.273) when primary children were asked to tackle a variety of word problems. They highlighted children's tendency to 'exclude' real world knowledge from school problems, possibly due to the stereotype problems that they usually experience in school, and the teaching and learning activities that take place around these. In the previous sections of this chapter, we highlighted ways of 'opening up' the mathematical activities that we use in the classroom, including providing more realistic activities that children can genuinely engage with. We will look at one more approach to mathematics in this section – the *realistic mathematics education* approach – which will provide further insights into how we might approach the issue of providing realistic experiences to children.

The development of the realistic mathematics education approach

Realistic mathematics education was an approach to teaching mathematics that was developed in the Netherlands in the 1960s and 1970s (Van den Heuvel-Panhuizen, 1998; Treffers and Beishuizen, 1999). This approach was greatly influenced by the Director of the IOWO Institute for the Development of Mathematics Education, Hans Freudenthal, with the institute subsequently being renamed the Freudenthal Institute in 1991. Freudenthal's view of mathematics was that it had to be connected to reality and to children's experiences of the real world for it to be useful to society (Van den Heuvel-Panhuizen, 1998). Freudenthal suggested that, for mathematicians, mathematics is the activity of doing mathematics, which involves their own organising of the mathematical ideas. Therefore, pupils of mathematics should be involved in the same type of activities (Gravemeijer, 1994). Mathematics should not just be seen as a subject to be transmitted, but a human activity where children are provided with opportunities, guided by the teacher, to 'reinvent' mathematics for themselves (Treffers and Beishuizen, 1999). In fact, the term 'realistic' has two possible meanings here. On the one hand, realistic mathematics education might involve examples of mathematical problems of what we would term the real world. On the other hand, the term 'realistic' in Dutch is closely related to the phrase 'to imagine'; therefore, realistic in this context means mathematical contexts that children can imagine for themselves (Van den Heuvel-Panhuizen, 2003).

Let us provide an initial example to illustrate these ideas. Treffers and Beishizen (1999) provide examples of children working on long-division problems. One of the questions they provide is *'64 pencils have to be packed in boxes of 16. How many boxes will be needed?'* (p. 30). They contrast solutions provided by British and Dutch children. The Dutch children opted straight away to tackle this, not by long division, but through multiplying 16 by small numbers and adding, ie 'chunking up' (eg 2 × 16 = 32, 2 × 16 = 32, 32 + 32 = 64). On the other hand, the British children were more likely to use a more traditional algorithm. In the example given by Treffers and Beishuizen for this particular question, the British child tried to use the 'bus stop' method:

$16\overline{)64}$

In fact, in the example from the British child, he/she tried this method, got it wrong, crossed it out, and then 'chunked up' in steps of 16.

```
36 × 10 = 360            36 | 1128              36 | 1128
36 × 10 = 360                 360   (10 buses)        1080   (30 buses)
360 + 360 = 720              ────                      ──
36 × 10 = 360                 768                      48
720 + 360 = 1080             360   (10 buses)          36   (1 bus)
1080 + 36 = 1116            ────                       ──
12 left over so 1 more bus    408                      12   (1 more bus)
10 + 10 + 10 + 1 +1 = 32 buses  360   (10 buses)
                            ────
                             48
                             36   (1 bus)
                            ──
                             12   (1 more bus)
```

Figure 7.8 *Range of solutions for a 'long-division' problem*

For Dutch children, the children's own methods are subsequently built upon by teachers through other problems. For example, for the problem *'1126 soldiers are transported on buses that have 36 seats. How many are needed?'* (Treffers and Beishuizen, 1999, p.29), we might see the range of solutions shown in Figure 7.8.

Some children may continue to chunk upwards. Other children, through guidance from the teacher, may be encouraged to use a different form of notation which resembles long division. Children in turn may make this more efficient so it closely resembles long division. But the important issue here is that children understand what they are doing as the methods have built on their own methods and existing understanding. Children are then encouraged to develop their understanding through 'guided' opportunities (not transmitted) and through opportunities to discuss with others and to metacognitively reflect on their own methods (Treffers and Beisguizen, 1999).

Mathematisation and models

The emphasis on discussion and reflection links strongly to the problem-solving processes that we have already discussed in this book. There are more connections we can make with issues we have discussed so far. With regards to children progressing in their understanding of problems and mathematical concepts, the realistic mathematics education approach places strong emphasis on the process of mathematisation that we discussed in the previous section. Therefore, in drawing on their own methods to tackle problems, children are being asked to mathematise the subject matter from realistic situations, and in turn to reflect and analyse their mathematisations (Gravemeijer, 1994). This idea is also developed further in realistic mathematics education. Van den Heuvel-Panhuizen (2003) highlights two ways of mathematising, and terms these *horizontal* and *vertical* mathematisation. Horizontal mathematisation is when *'mathematical tools are brought forward and used to organize and solve a problem situated in daily life'* (p.12). Therefore, the examples that we saw in the mathematical modelling section would be examples of the horizontal process, where we represent the real world with symbols. Alternatively vertical mathematisation *'stands for all kinds of re-organizations and operations done by the students within the mathematical system itself'* (p.12). This may be part of the reflective processes where we refine the way we have represented the real world symbolically. The possible progression in the way we represent long division as shown in Figure 7.8 is an example of this. Therefore, once again, realistic mathematics education emphasises the representational and reflective processes involved in our mathematical thinking.

Connecting further to the idea of mathematical thinking, Gravemeijer (1999) emphasises the role of 'models' in realistic mathematics education. In traditional approaches to mathematics teaching, models, or what we would call external representations, are used to make the mathematical ideas more 'concrete' for children. These models are part of the mathematics that children need to come to understand. In realistic mathematics education, however, the emphasis is on children developing their own models. As Gravemeijer (1999) states:

> *'the models are grounded in the contextual problems that are to be solved by the students. The models in (realistic mathematics education) are related to modeling; the starting point is in the contextual situation of the problem that has to be solved. This problem is modeled by the students who solve it with help of the construed model. The premise here is that students who work with these models will be encouraged to (re)invent the more formal mathematics.'*
>
> (p.159)

As stated before, the children are then guided by the teacher to refine their models in a process of vertical mathematisation. An example of this is the empty number line. The empty number line was developed in the realistic mathematics education approach as a means of supporting flexible approaches to computation (Gravemeijer, 1999). However, in supporting children to use the empty number line, the teacher may start with counting objects, then perhaps counting on a bead string, then progress onto the empty number line (Figure 7.9). The bead string might provide a model which children can more closely identify with, and then build upon and refine this model to develop an understanding of the empty number line.

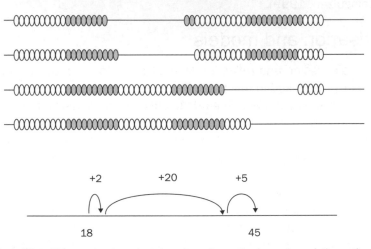

Figure 7.9 *Adding 18 + 27 on the bead string (top four diagrams) and then the empty number line (bottom diagram)*

The emphasis in realistic mathematics education is that we move from realistic experiences for the children and refine the models that they use through teacher guidance. We might contrast this with the approach that is very often taken in English classrooms where there is less clear progression in the use of the number line (Murphy, 2011), hoping instead that children will unproblematically understand this external representation. In fact, this approach with models and mathematisation provides an important distinction for realistic mathematics education. Whereas previously, for example in investigations or mathematical modelling, although there was an emphasis on representation and reflection, the focus was more on the particular rich mathematical activity and how understanding can be developed from it. In realistic mathematics education, however, the emphasis is on how particular mathematical concepts can be taught, using problems as a vehicle for encouraging children (Van den Heuvel-Panhuizen, 2003). Therefore, problems are part of a 'learning trajectory' where learning opportunities for children are developed through the careful sequencing of problems. Therefore, although we are drawing on the same problem-solving processes highlighted throughout the book, realistic mathematics education involves a 'longitudinal' perspective on developing understanding through the use of realistic problems (Van den Heuvel-Panhuizen, 2003).

An example from the UK

Let us provide one final example of this type of approach to illustrate the above ideas, and also to show the possible benefits of such an approach for children. Here in the UK, a lot of work in implementing realistic mathematics education, particularly in secondary schools, has been carried out by Manchester Metropolitan University. Building on work carried out in the United States at the University of Wisconsin-Madison (see their *Mathematics in Context* webpage at http://showmecenter.missouri.edu/showme/mic.shtml for numerous examples and further details), researchers at Manchester Metropolitan University have trialled *Mathematics in Context* materials in local schools since 2003. Dickinson and Eade (2005) provide examples of realistic contexts which were used in these secondary schools to develop children's understanding of fractions (Figure 7.10).

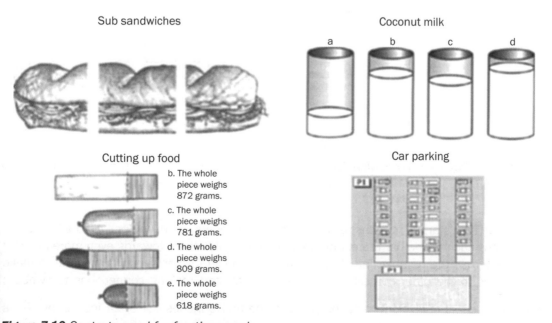

Figure 7.10 *Contexts used for fractions work*

So, an initial contextualised problem might be *'Three friends have enough to buy two sub sandwiches. Each sub sandwich is 24 inches long. What fraction of a sub sandwich will each friend get? How long in total will their piece or pieces of sandwich be?'* In answering this question, it is hoped that the context will encourage children to develop a 'bar' model of fractions (Figure 7.11).

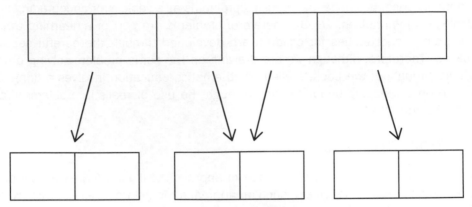

Figure 7.11 *Bar model of fractions for the given problem*

Dickinson and Eade (2005) also show the possible refinement of this initial fraction model in what they call the *'progressive formalisation of models'* (p.5) (Figure 7.12).

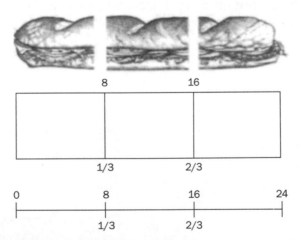

Figure 7.12 *Progressive formalisation of the fraction model (Figures 7.10 and 7.12 were used with kind permission from Paul Dickinson at Manchester Metropolitan University)*

We can see that, starting from the sandwich context, teachers can build upon children's models for fractions such as the bar representation, and then guide them towards even more abstract models such as the number line. The number line model further supports children to make connections to the other contexts for fractions, or to start making connections to symbolic concepts such as equivalent fractions (we can see that 8 inches out of 24 inches, or $\dfrac{8}{24}$ is equivalent to $\frac{1}{3}$). Therefore, through the use of problems contextualised in meaningful contexts for children, the teacher can build up their models or representations, and use these to further develop their understanding of a mathematical concept.

We can demonstrate these benefits through the results of an evaluation of Manchester Metropolitan University's realistic mathematics education project. One of the authors of the present book was involved in the analysis of data obtained from Key Stage 3 pupils in 12 secondary schools involved in the project (Dickinson et al, 2011). There was also a matched control group of pupils not involved in the project. A test consisting of nine questions, looking at pupils' abilities both to solve a variety of problems and also to explain their solutions, was used to assess the impact of the project. An example of one of the questions, taken from Dickinson and Eade (2005), is shown below (Figure 7.13).

Find the area of the shape shown below.
Show carefully how you worked it out

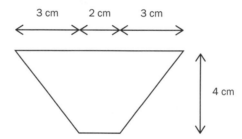

Figure 7.13 *Example of a test question from the realistic mathematics education evaluation*

In assessing pupils' answers, these were judged in two ways. Firstly they were judged in terms of whether the answer given was correct or not. Secondly, the quality of explanation in each case was categorised (in order of quality of explanations) as: (a) no explanation; (b) an incorrect explanation or diagram; (c) a reasonable diagram or a correct explanation; and (d) a reasonable diagram and a correct explanation. It was found that the project pupils got more correct answers than the control group pupils on each of the test questions except one. In addition, however, the overall quality of explanations by the project pupils was better for every question compared to the control group pupils.

We can explain these results in terms of the realistic mathematics education approach. An important part of the approach is to encourage children to develop their own models or representations for mathematical concepts, and in turn to reflect and to refine these models. These models are used in the mathematical thinking of children. Therefore, it seems reasonable that children show more advanced abilities to explain their ideas in terms of the representations and the thinking involved. This links back once again to the important problem-solving processes that have underpinned this book.

Critical questions

» Have you used or experienced any of the sorts of ideas promoted by the realistic mathematics education approach?

» Although schools and teachers may face constraints in extensively implementing a realistic mathematics education approach, how could you incorporate elements of the approach into your teaching? What areas of mathematics might you use and what models could you focus on?

Open approaches to mathematics: the classroom perspective

Examining the issues regarding open approaches to mathematics from a classroom perspective, we suggest that open-ended problems and investigations can be presented to children in different ways:

- with very little structure or guidance, allowing children the opportunity to interpret and respond in different ways;

- with a high degree of initial structure and/or guidance, allowing the teacher to shape the route and outcome;

- somewhere between these two extremes.

It can be quite difficult, if the teacher is used to providing closed problems and structured lessons, to relinquish control and present activities with little guidance. What happens if children take the activity in a direction you hadn't anticipated? What if they then ask a question that you aren't prepared for and cannot answer? We would suggest that if your classroom ethos is one that genuinely promotes learning, encourages a 'have a go' mentality and values the insights gained from mistakes, then that should also be true for you as the teacher. It is a powerful message to children that we never stop learning and that teachers are not the fountain of all knowledge. How powerful to a child's confidence it is to work on something with the teacher and overcome the problem together!

How a problem or investigation is presented to children will determine their level of autonomy and consequently the quality of predictions, hypotheses and understanding. Open problems and investigations presented with little guidance allow children to develop their own mathematical ideas and to explore different approaches. This, coupled with valuable discussion, reasoning and justification, amounts to a rich learning opportunity. Groups might find a solution or solutions to the problem, which may lead to a generalisation; they might find a rule or pattern that can be explored further or they may indeed come to no conclusion or final solution at all – these outcomes are all legitimate. The value of using open problems and investigations this way lies in the journey of problem solving and open approaches to mathematics; the concepts and skills that have been acquired and practised along the way, and not in arriving at the 'correct' answer predetermined by restrictions laid out by the teacher in the initial stages.

Though we are talking here about presenting activities with less guidance and structure, this does not mean that lesson planning is any less necessary. A plan for lessons of this type will not have each stage of learning identified, nor is it likely to have differentiated activities; the maths used will be determined by the children's choices and the differentiation will be apparent in their outcomes. A good plan, however, should show that the teacher has thought out the stages children will work through. It may contain key questions which very much reflect the important problem-solving processes that we have highlighted so far. For example:

If children have difficulty accessing the problem or investigation:

•   What do you know already?

•   Could you represent the problem a different way?

•   Are there any resources that might help?

•   Have you talked it through as a group and shared your thoughts?

If children are stuck:

•   What have you done so far?

•   What do you know now?

•   What do you want to know?

•   How else could you represent the problem?

•   What else could you work out?

•   Are you being systematic?

•   Have you encountered this type of problem before?

To move learning on:

•   What if...?

•   What else can you find out?

When a solution or solutions are found, or at the end of the activity:

•   Review your work – what would you do differently next time?

•   Could you have been more systematic?

•   Can you identify an alternative approach? Is it more efficient than the route you took?

•   Can you explain your reasoning to others?

•   Could you identify what type of problem this was and did that help?

•   What have you learned previously that helped you today?

•   What have you learned from this activity?

You should also plan for the questions you will ask yourself at the end of the activity:

- Were there any common misconceptions?
- If children were stuck, was it because of their maths subject knowledge or was it because of their ability to solve problems?
- Did particular stages of the activity cause confusion?
- Were there any common questions of adults?
- Did children know what to do if they were stuck?
- Did they work as a team and discuss ideas?
- Were children creative in their approach?
- Were they systematic?
- Did children use mathematical vocabulary appropriately?
- Could children reflect on the process?
- Could children explain their reasoning clearly to others?
- What have I learned about children's ability to solve problems?

If children are used to lots of guidance and/or closed problems, it may be wise to introduce open-ended problems and less guidance in a controlled manner. Also remember that, even if the problem or investigation has been presented with very little structure initially, further guidance can be given later in the lesson to particular groups, if that will promote learning and increase mathematical confidence.

Critical questions

» *Have you experienced any whole-school approaches to incorporating more open approaches to mathematics in classrooms? If so, how successful were these and what kinds of approaches were incorporated?*

» *In your experience, what constraints do schools face in developing open approaches to mathematics?*

» *Are open approaches to mathematics more suitable for children of particular abilities or ages, or do you think they are suitable across the board?*

Critical reflections

In this chapter, what we have tried to do is to 'open out' our view of problem solving to include other approaches. It may be that approaches such as mathematical modelling or realistic mathematics education are unusual in terms of their use in primary classrooms in the UK. However, even with investigative activities, we have seen from the research that there is reluctance by teachers to use such an approach. What we have tried to show in this chapter is that, essentially, apart from focussing a little more on particular aspects, any of the open approaches described involve the fundamental processes of problem solving that we have emphasised so much in this book. In fact, we would say that it is not really about which approach you take; rather it is about using activities that genuinely call upon children to use all aspects of the problem-solving processes. Hopefully, we have also shown how opening out our approach to the teaching and learning of mathematics leads us into interesting directions, and we will consider this issue of interest, or engagement, in the next chapter.

In trying to illustrate the extent to which all these open approaches are connected, we want to emphasise other connections as well. We have already said that we will look in the next chapter at the issues of engagement and enrichment which underpin all our open approaches. Also, we would consider that all of these approaches call upon creative skills from both children and teachers. We emphasise too that although the last chapter was entitled 'assessing problem solving', actually, as we saw from some of the assessment approaches that we identified, and also the underpinning of the assessment process by our general processes linked to problem solving, our conclusions from the last chapter would apply also to the open approaches described. What we think is exciting is the way that focussing on the fundamental processes allows us to make all these connections between areas that we may have seen as separate before. We hope this ability also allows you to make connections between activities and observations that you see taking place in the classroom.

Taking it further

For a good, broad and not overly long discussion of open approaches to mathematics, we would recommend the article by Pehkonen (1997). In terms of particular open approaches, Ponte and Lesh have written extensively on investigations and mathematical modelling respectively, although we would also recommend English and Watters (2005) for a primary perspective on mathematical modelling. Looking at the historical and theoretical background to realistic mathematics education, Treffers and Beishuizen (1999) and Van den Heuvel-Panhuizen (1998) both provide accessible descriptions.

English, L D, & Watters, J J (2005) Mathematical modelling in the early school years. *Mathematics Education Research Journal*, 16(3): 58–79

Pehkonen, E (1997) The state-of-art in mathematical creativity. *ZDM*, 29(3), 63–67

Ponte, J P (2007) Investigations and explorations in the mathematics classroom. *ZDM*, 39(5), 419–430

Lesh, R & Doerr, H M (2003) Foundations of models and modeling perspectives on mathematics teaching, learning, and problem solving, in Lesh, R & Doerr, H (eds) *Beyond constructivism: models and modeling perspectives on mathematics problem solving, learning, and teaching* (pp. 3–33). Mahwah, NJ: Lawrence Erlbaum Associates Inc

Treffers, A & Beishuizen, M (1999) Realistic mathematics education in the Netherlands, in Thompson, I (ed) *Issues in teaching numeracy in primary schools* (pp. 27–38). Buckingham: Open University Press

Van den Heuvel-Panhuizen, M (1998) Realistic Mathematics Education as work in progress, in Lin, F L (ed) *Common sense in mathematics education: proceedings of 2001 the Netherlands and Taiwan conference on mathematics education* (pp. 1–43). Taipei, Taiwan, 19–23 November 2001

8 Enrichment and engagement with problem solving

Key issues in this chapter

- This chapter links the problem-solving processes, including the open approaches to mathematics that we covered in the last chapter, to the notion of enriching children's experiences of mathematics, and in turn engaging them in the subject.

- It carefully explains what is meant by 'enrichment'. Very often, enrichment is associated with provision for higher attaining children. This chapter provides examples of enrichment activities that can be used with higher attaining and other children, contrasting this to the notion of acceleration. It also makes links to cross-curricular or multi-cultural approaches to mathematics to support this enrichment process.

- It specifically defines what is meant by engagement. Perhaps the most critical factor in engaging children is providing them with activities that make them think. It is therefore not just about 'fun activities'. This link with thinking leads back to the thinking and reasoning aspects of the problem solving processes, and the chapter concludes that genuine problem-solving activities (or more open activities) will therefore most likely lead to child engagement.

Introduction

The introduction to this book highlighted a number of clear advantages to incorporating problem solving into your teaching. One of these was the positive impact problem-solving activities can have on children's attitudes toward and perspectives on mathematics. This chapter looks at this issue of engagement in mathematics in much more detail, through examining how problem solving can be used to enrich the mathematical experiences of children. In doing so, it refers back to the processes of problem solving detailed earlier in the book, and also the more 'open' problem-solving approaches, such as investigations, detailed in the last chapter. It clarifies what is meant by enrichment and engagement, and why these should be desirable characteristics of mathematics teaching.

Enrichment in mathematics

In reading this book, you may have noticed the importance we place on first defining exactly what we mean when discussing particular concepts, eg a problem, problem solving, etc. We feel this is important because one person's notion of a particular concept can often be different to another's and 'singing from different hymn sheets' is not productive. We try to do the same here in discussing the issue of enrichment. Feng (2006) put forward four 'paradigmatic positions' on enrichment in order to summarise the different types of mathematical activities that are included under the umbrella of 'enrichment'.

1. Development of mathematical talent, including extending mathematical skills and heightening interest in the subject.

2. Popular contextualisation of the subject, including tackling negative stereotypes and deepening mathematical understanding.

3. Enhancement of mathematical learning processes, including developing learning skills.

4. Outreach to the mathematically underprivileged, including widening student access to mathematics.

These different views of enrichment can be used as a starting point for exploring enrichment and for providing examples. Piggott (2004) provided the example of the NRICH project run by the University of Cambridge. In the previous chapter on open approaches to mathematics related to problem solving, we drew on the example provided by NRICH for an investigation into mathematics. The project described by Piggott involved an online community based around the NRICH resources, providing 'able' children with the access to mathematical activities. In trying to conceptualise the important characteristics of such enrichment activities, Piggott (2004) emphasised the crucial role played by problem solving and mathematical thinking in the enrichment process. This relates very strongly to what we have already discussed in this book. Such an enrichment activity concurs with a number of Feng's (2006) perspectives, eg providing for talented children, widening access to mathematics and developing learning processes such as mathematical thinking.

An example of an enrichment activity – The Eye of Horus

To provide a clearer example of such enrichment activities, we can draw on our own experiences of working with Year 5 and Year 6 children in what we termed 'enrichment' sessions. Primary schools in the authors' local area were invited to send approximately five children each to planned enrichment sessions run on a Saturday morning. These sessions were held in a university lecture theatre and designed to challenge and enthuse primary children in mathematics by providing activities that allowed children to apply their knowledge of mathematics in a broader context, and to develop their knowledge and thinking skills as they applied this knowledge. Around 100 children attended each of two enrichment sessions run in 2012–13. One activity involved children exploring the 'Eye of Horus'. Horus was one of the gods from Ancient Egypt, very often represented as a falcon. In one of the stories from Ancient Egypt, Horus and his brother Set fought, resulting in Set gouging out one of Horus' eyes and tearing it to pieces. This eye was pieced back together by another Egyptian god, and as a result, the Eye of Horus was used in Ancient Egypt as a way of representing parts of a whole or fractions in mathematics. Figure 8.1 shows a typical diagram detailing the relationship between the Eye of Horus and fractions. Each different part of the eye represented a different unit fraction; for example the pupil of the eye represented $\frac{1}{4}$ whereas the brow of the eye represented $\frac{1}{8}$. Other fractions could be represented by drawing and highlighting combinations of different parts of the eye. For example, highlighting the pupil and the eye brow together would represent $\frac{1}{4} + \frac{1}{8} = \frac{5}{8}$.

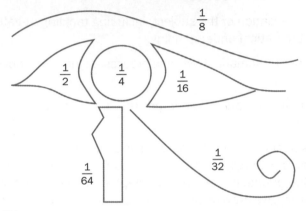

Figure 8.1 *The Eye of Horus*

The broader aim of the enrichment session was to enrich the experiences of the Year 5 and 6 children in fractions, in order to develop their understanding of fractions further. Therefore, using the above starting point, we asked the children to consider the following questions.

• How much do the fractions in the Eye of Horus add up to? Did the other Egyptian god pick up all the bits or did she miss a bit?

• How could you show $\frac{5}{8}$ or $\frac{11}{32}$ or $\frac{15}{16}$?

We provided the children with sheets containing the above diagram so that they could simply show different fractions by drawing over the diagram. In asking the children to tackle these questions, we linked back to activities that we had done on adding fractions using equivalent fractions, and ways of representing fractions. An extension question that we asked the children was *'How many different fractions could you show on one picture of the eye of Horus?'* Here, the emphasis was on the children's thinking as they tackled the problem, encouraging systematic approaches and generalising in trying to cover all the combinations. A possible approach to this problem might look something like this. We can simply list the different combinations that we can get with six parts, making sure we do not repeat a given part in any combination (you cannot use one part of the eye twice in a fraction). So, instead of the fractions, we could just call them a, b, c, d, e and f and show the possible combinations of these six parts. We clearly have six combinations when we have just one part (a, b, c, d, e, f). If we have two parts, we have the following combinations:

ab, ac, ad, ae, af (5)

bc, bd, be, bf (4)

cd, ce, cf (3)

de, df (2)

ef (1)

or a total of 15. With three parts, we have the combinations:

abc, abd, abe, abf, acd, ace, acf, ade, adf, aef (4 + 3 + 2 + 1 = 10)

bcd, bce, bcf, bde, bdf, bef (3 + 2 + 1 = 6)

cde, cdf, cef (2 + 1 = 3)

def (1)

or a total of 20. With four parts, we have the combinations:

abcd, abce, abcf, abde, abdf, abef, acde, acdf, acef, adef (6 + 3 + 1 = 10)

bcde, bcdf, bcef, bdef (3 + 1 = 4)

cdef (1)

or a total of 15. With five parts, we hope you can see the pattern that we would get is 4 + 1 = 5 and 1 making a total of 6. With six parts, we would just get 1. Therefore, in total we get 6 + 15 + 20 + 15 + 6 + 1 = 63. Interestingly, we can look at this in another way. If we start to add different combinations of fractions:

$$\frac{1}{2}$$

$$\frac{1}{2}+\frac{1}{4}=\frac{2}{4}+\frac{1}{4}=\frac{3}{4}$$

$$\frac{1}{2}+\frac{1}{8}=\frac{4}{8}+\frac{1}{8}=\frac{5}{8}$$

$$\frac{1}{4}+\frac{1}{8}=\frac{2}{8}+\frac{1}{8}=\frac{3}{8}$$

We may start to see another pattern. In order to get a total with a denominator of 2, only

$\frac{1}{2}$ can contribute to that. For a total with denominator 4, $\frac{1}{2}$ and $\frac{1}{4}$ can contribute to that to

give 2 combinations that cannot be simplified (with numerators 1 and 3 – odd numbers not exceeding the denominator). For a total with denominator 8, $\frac{1}{2}$, $\frac{1}{4}$ and $\frac{1}{8}$ can contribute to that to give 4 combinations that cannot be simplified (with numerators 1, 3, 5, 7). For a total with denominator 16, we would have numerators 1, 3, 5, 7, 9, 11, 13, 15; that's 8 combinations. For a total with denominator 32, we would have 16 combinations. For a total with denominator 64, we would have 32 combinations. We would therefore have 1 + 2 + 4 + 8 + 16 + 32 = 63 combinations in total. Looking in detail at these combinations, we seem to cover all the fractions with a denominator of 64, even those with even numerators that can be simplified to fractions with smaller denominators. You can hopefully see that the Eye of Horus activity is a rich problem for exploring and manipulating fractions, with wider connections to ways in which fractions were represented in the past. In terms of Feng's different perspectives on enrichment activities outlined above, we would argue that the enrichment sessions with local Year 5 and 6 children covered all four of the possible perspectives on enrichment.

An example of an enrichment activity – master classes

Let us examine another example of an enrichment activity in mathematics. In 2008, one of the authors of the present book was involved in an evaluation of the Royal Institution's secondary mathematics master classes programme (some details of the evaluation are provided in Santos and Barmby, 2010). Like the enrichment activities detailed above (which in fact were based on the Royal Institution's master classes model), the secondary master classes took place on Saturdays, with the objectives of developing children's attitudes in mathematics and to get them doing mathematics through meaningfully contextualised tasks. A further objective of the master classes was to provide professional development opportunities for teachers accompanying their children. In fact, details of both the primary and secondary master classes run by the Royal Institution, with resources for teachers, are given on their website (www. rigb.org/education/masterclasses/master class-resources, accessed 30th December 2013). Let us take one of the primary topics that they use for the masterclasses as an example. A possible investigation involves the Platonic solids. A Platonic solid is a 3D shape comprising faces made of congruent regular 2D shapes, where the same number of 2D shapes meet at each vertex. An example of a Platonic solid is the cube (or hexahedron), consisting of squares for each face, with three squares meeting at each vertex (Figure 8.2).

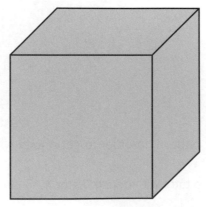

Figure 8.2 *A cube (or hexahedron)*

A possible starting point for such an investigation would be to see how regular 2D shapes tessellate on a flat surface. Starting off with equilateral triangles, we see that six equilateral triangles tessellate. In turn, four squares tessellate and three hexagons tessellate also (Figure 8.3). A question we could ask of children is why we do not have any other combinations of regular 2D shapes tessellating. Moving on then to 3D shapes, we can consider how regular 2D shapes fit around a vertex, rather than on a flat surface. In the Royal Institution example, children use cut out shapes or other physical resources to see how regular 2D shapes fit around a vertex. We find the following possible combinations (Table 8.1).

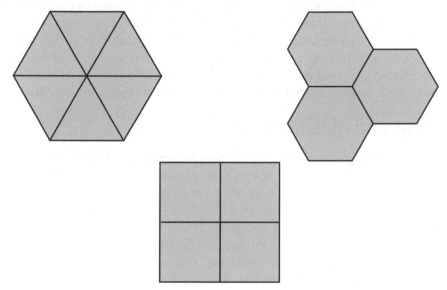

Figure 8.3 *Tessellating regular 2D shapes*

Table 8.1 *Possible Platonic solids*

	Regular 2D shapes (with each individual internal angle)			
	Triangle	**Square**	**Pentagon**	**Hexagon**
Number at vertex	(60°)	(90°)	(108°)	(120°)
3	Tetrahedron	Cube	Dodecahedron	-
4	Octahedron	-	-	-
5	Icosahedron	-	-	-
6	-	-	-	-

When we move from tessellating 2D shapes on a flat surface to fitting 2D shapes around a vertex, the available angle that we have for fitting the shapes together is reduced. We therefore cannot have three hexagons fitting around a vertex as they already take up 360° on a flat surface. We can fit three pentagons (although they would not tessellate on a flat surface due to their internal angles), three squares and three triangles (none of which would exceed 360° on a flat surface). We cannot fit four squares or pentagons as the internal angles are too great. However, we can fit four or five triangles. We cannot fit six triangles, again because the internal angles are too great. Therefore, in total, there are only five Platonic solids. The above is the kind of thinking that we might hope for from children as a result of their practical investigation into 2D shapes. As emphasised by the objectives of the Royal Institution's master classes, by 'doing' such mathematical activities, it is hoped that children are 'engaged' by the mathematics, and that their understanding of the mathematical concepts are developed through such activities. We might ask why such activities would be 'engaging' to children, and we will try and answer that question shortly. However, before we do so, let us make a couple of additional connections to the idea of enrichment.

Enrichment and able children

In Feng's (2006) paradigm, related to enrichment activities, the first perspective related to working with children who are more able in mathematics. Indeed, in both the enrichment activities detailed above, although it was not a condition that only the most able children attend the enrichment sessions, schools were more likely to put forward their higher attaining children in mathematics. Indeed, we can make the connection between enrichment and the recommendations from research for supporting more able children in mathematics. In talking about 'more able' or 'higher attaining' children we must be careful as to what we mean by these terms. Krutestkii (1976) identified a number of characteristics which he associated with 'gifted' pupils of mathematics. In addition to characteristics such as having a good memory for mathematical facts, these also included being logical, systematic, concise and flexible in their mathematical thinking processes. The characteristics also involved being able to extract the mathematical structure from given problems, and being able to represent concepts using symbols and numbers. Threlfall (2010) identified characteristics such as an interconnected knowledge base, efficiency at representing problems, flexibility in strategies for problem solving, and sophisticated metacognition and self-regulation skills. Orton (2004) made a similar point with regards to metacognition:

> *Mathematically-able pupils adopt a procedure in solving mathematical problems which suggests they can follow a plan which involves trying out ideas systematically and in which they appear to be able to see which ideas are worth pursuing and which are not.*

> (p.143)

All these characteristics of more able or gifted pupils in mathematics relate to the problem-solving processes and skills that we have identified in this book.

If these are the important skills that need developing in such children, then we need to provide opportunities for these children in which this development can take place. Koshy

(2003) specifically states that children will only show special talent in mathematics if they are given opportunities to do so. This leads to implications for working with more able children in mathematics. Government guidelines in the past have suggested both acceleration of children in mathematics (eg provision of learning objectives from higher year groups, or actually working in higher year groups) and enrichment of the children's mathematical experiences (DfES, 2000). This is supported by the research:

> ... services for our most promising students should not only look at changing the rate of presentation or the number of the mathematical topics, but must also look at changing the depth or complexities of the mathematical investigations. Promising students should be encouraged to take time to explore the depth and complexities of problems, their patterns, and connections among them.

(Sheffield, 1999, p.16)

We sometimes concentrate solely on accelerating children in their mathematical learning. However, the reason for providing such enrichment activities in mathematics is so that we cater more broadly for the needs of able children in the subject.

Enrichment in the classroom

It is important that we make an additional connection to the issue of enrichment. In the discussion so far in this chapter, we have used examples of enrichment activities taking place outside of the everyday classroom. However, we must emphasise that this need not be the case. Rather, what we want to promote is the use of 'enrichment' activities within the classroom. In doing so, we encourage teachers to use the problems, investigations and other more 'open' approaches to mathematics that we have outlined so far in the book. In both the quotes outlined above by Orton and Sheffield, the importance of mathematical problems for the enriching of children's mathematical experiences is emphasised. Certainly, in terms of Feng's paradigms, we have underlined the role that problem solving serves in terms of developing children's mathematical understanding and developing their learning/thinking skills. We can also go a step further and say that, in encouraging you to enrich your teaching of the subject, we are asking you to think about how you can *teach creatively* in mathematics. In the chapter on creativity and problem solving, we emphasised the distinction between *teaching for creativity* and *teaching creatively*, with the latter being *'teachers using imaginative approaches to make learning more interesting, exciting and effective'* (NACCCE, 1999, p.102). Therefore, from the perspective of mathematics learning being more engaging, we want you to incorporate more creative ways of teaching the subject.

Let us provide an example to illustrate this. We emphasised before that the notion of creativity involves making connections to new areas and also reviewing the value of this connection. Therefore, we want our teaching to connect the learning of mathematics to areas outside of what we might cover normally. That may be cross-curricular approaches to teaching the subject, similar to the Eye of Horus example above. Another example, again from the context of Ancient Egypt, is provided by Joseph (1991). If we multiply 225 by 17, we can do it by writing down the multiplier (in this case 17) and successively doubling this.

1	17
2	34
4	68
8	136
16	272
32	544
64	1088
128	2176
256	4352

We can see that 256 'lots' of 17 is 4352 but this is too much. We only want 225 times 17. If we go back up the list and successively add the left-hand column numbers without going over 225, we get 128 + 64 + 32 + 1 = 225. We therefore have to add the corresponding right hand column numbers: 2176 + 1088 + 544 + 17 = 3825. In our teaching, we might introduce this Egyptian method of multiplication, not because we want children to use it instead of our traditional long multiplication algorithm (although they may do). Rather, it is interesting to consider why this works. In considering this problem, children may explore ideas around the distributive law in multiplication, and therefore deepen their understanding of the operation.

Teaching creatively therefore can potentially lead to the enrichment of mathematical learning for children and, we hope, deepen their understanding of the mathematics involved and develop their mathematical thinking. But what of the other aspects of enrichment discussed earlier, particularly in terms of developing children's attitudes, interest and engagement? We will now turn our attention to this issue of engagement.

Critical questions

» *From your own experience, what enrichment activities in mathematics have the children that you have worked with experienced? What were the characteristics of these activities that associated them with enrichment?*

» *Once again, from your experience, have the enrichment activities that you have come across been reserved for more able children? Or did a greater range of children take part? What might be the arguments for and against incorporating a large range of child abilities?*

» *In your experience, are enrichment activities part of the everyday classroom, or are they carried out separately? If the latter, what might be the implications of this?*

» *In thinking about the discussion on enrichment activities given above, can you think of ways in which you could enrich your everyday teaching of mathematics? What topics might you focus on?*

Engagement in mathematics

In the same way as we did for enrichment, let us begin by trying to define what we mean by 'engagement'. Fortunately, the research literature on engagement generally (not just in maths) provides a clear description of the construct. Newmann et al (1992) defined engagement as *'students' psychological investment in and effort directed toward learning, understanding, or mastering the knowledge, skills, or crafts that academic work is intended to promote'* (p.12). As with enrichment therefore, we see a close connection between engagement and the notion of developing understanding. In fact, in mathematics, researchers have highlighted the importance of child engagement because of its relationship to the academic attainment of learners (Peterson and Fennema, 1985; Park 2005). We can go into greater detail on this definition of engagement. Research has proposed that there are three 'dimensions' to engagement: the cognitive dimension, the affective dimension, and the behavioural dimension (Fredericks et al, 2004; Kong et al, 2003). Cognitive engagement is the 'psychological investment' mentioned previously, and in fact Meece et al (1988) stated that this cognitive engagement involves the learners' metacognition and self-regulation strategies. Affective or emotional engagement relates to the way we feel about being involved in a particular task. Behavioural engagement is the way we behave towards the given task. Munns and Woodford (2006) therefore summarise that:

> *... the term engagement should be reserved specifically for learning situations where the cognitive, emotional and behavioural components are all strongly present at the same time ... . Viewed in this way, student engagement is when students are simultaneously:*

> • *reflectively involved in deep understanding and expertise (high cognition);*

> • *genuinely valuing what they are doing (high emotion);*

> • *actively participating in school and classroom activities (high behaviour).*

> (p.194)

We find from the research literature that the notion of 'attitude' is also defined in a similar way, involving cognitive, affective and behavioural dimensions (Crano and Prislin, 2006).

From the definition above, we see that feelings about and behaviour towards mathematical tasks are part of this notion of engagement in mathematics, but we would particularly emphasise here the need for children to be cognitively engaged as well. In fact, we would suggest that this is the most important dimension – in order for children to genuinely be behaviourally engaged, they need to be thinking about the mathematical task. If the task does not require much thinking, then their participation in the task is short-lived. In turn, tasks which are cognitively engaging lead to emotional engagement. In our experience of enrichment sessions, the enjoyment does not necessarily come from 'fun activities'. Appropriately cognitively demanding activities also provide this affective engagement. This leads us to an explanation of why enrichment activities, and by implication problem-solving and other 'open' mathematical activities, promote child engagement. As we have seen from the problem-solving processes described previously, if a problem is, by definition, to be a problem to a child, it must result in them thinking about how to tackle it. If they are involved in this process of thinking then they are engaged cognitively, behaviourally and, we hope, emotionally in the task.

We have therefore shown the close link between enrichment and engagement. In fact, this close link led to Santos and Barmby (2010) putting forward a more concise definition of what we mean by enrichment activities in mathematics. Enrichment is simply mathematical activities that result in the engagement of learners. And if this engagement is taking place, then the learners are thinking through the mathematical tasks, and are therefore more likely to develop their understanding. We can see that this rather simple definition covers Feng's (2006) paradigms for enrichment (in terms of cognitive, affective and behavioural aspects), and also further emphasises the importance of incorporating problem-solving activities in our teaching. And, once again, we emphasise that enrichment is not something that is external to what we do in the classroom. Rather, through activities that cognitively engage children such as problem-solving tasks, or developing child understanding through teaching creatively, we can enrich children's experiences of mathematics and develop their engagement in the subject.

Critical questions

» *Think about times when you have observed children being really engaged in mathematical activities. What was it about the activities that really engaged them? Can you use the cognitive, affective and behavioural view of engagement to suggest which of these aspects are the most important for children that you work with?*

» *Thinking about problem solving or open approaches to mathematics that you have used in the classroom, have these indeed led to greater engagement during the activities? If so, what was it about these activities that led to engagement?*

» *What are some of the possible barriers to engaging children in mathematical activities?*

Critical reflections

In this chapter, as throughout the book, we have taken the concepts under discussion, used the available research, and tried to pin down more specifically what we mean by these concepts. In doing so, we make connections to other related concepts, and therefore, we start to build up the bigger conceptual picture. And so it is with enrichment and engagement. Before the start of the chapter, you may have had a particular notion of what these concepts mean. Certainly, for us researching these ideas, we had prior conceptions based on our experiences. However, in exploring these issues in detail, we hope you have developed the way you look at these issues.

For example, with regards to enrichment, consider how enrichment in mathematics is incorporated in your school. In our experiences, enrichment is very often associated with activities outside the everyday primary classroom. It is the same with engagement. Prior to reading this chapter, in what ways did you think about and discuss engagement? Again, from our experiences, engagement is often associated with 'unusual' activities, activities which are not part of our everyday teaching of mathematics.

What we hope we have shown in the chapter is that, if we incorporate genuine problem-solving activities in our teaching, and of course this includes the open approaches detailed in the last chapter, then we are likely to be enriching children's experiences in mathematics and engaging them in the subject. These activities are not something special that we need to reserve for special occasions; rather, we can frequently incorporate these ideas in our teaching. Therefore, in your own context of teaching, using the theoretical as well as the practical ideas in this chapter, consider how you and your colleagues can further enrich your teaching and engage the children.

In doing so, you should bear in mind one possible obstacle. As we highlighted in the chapter on assessment, a frequent reason for not engaging in problem-solving activities is the difficulty of assessing children in these activities. We have shown that this is possible, if we focus on the processes involved. Likewise, if we are using such activities to engage children and enrich their experiences, this does not mean that this excludes assessing the children. Therefore, when using such activities in your teaching, keep this in mind, and try to assess the progress your children are making in the processes they are using. In this way, you can still look to develop their mathematical thinking and problem-solving skills, while possibly improving children's views of the subject. We hope, in this way, that everyone wins!

Taking it further

In terms of studying further the issue of enrichment in mathematics, as was highlighted in the chapter, there is not actually a wealth of research out there on this topic. However, we would point people to the work of Feng, and also once again to the work of the NRICH project based at the University of Cambridge, which Piggott (2004) has been involved in. In terms of engagement, there is a great deal more literature available. We would suggest as a starting point the overview by Newmann et al (1992), which is available as a download.

Feng, W Y (2010) Students' experience of mathematics enrichment. *Paper presented at the 7th British conference in mathematics education, University of Manchester*

Piggott, J (2004) Mathematical enrichment: what is it and who is it for? *Paper presented at BERA conference, Manchester, September* 2004

Newmann, F M, Wehlage, G G, & Lamborn, S D (1992) The significance and sources of student engagement, in Newmann, F M (ed) *Student engagement and achievement in American secondary school* (pp. 11–39). New York: Teachers College Press

Conclusion

We have now reached the end of our considerations with regards to problem solving, and how we can support its teaching and learning in schools. But, before we finish, let us look back and consider how we have approached this whole topic of problem solving, and the important issues that we want readers to take away with them and apply in schools. In some ways, this book has been a journey of exploration through problem solving, and concepts and ideas related to problem solving. Therefore, let us examine the journey we have taken (Figure 9.1).

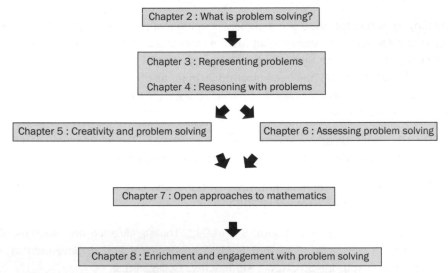

Figure 9.1 *The journey through problem solving undertaken in the book*

If there is one key idea that we would like you to take away from this book, it is being clear about what we mean by problem solving. More specifically, when we ask children (or anyone for that matter) to problem solve, what do we want to encourage them to do? Starting in

Chapter 2, an issue that we have emphasised throughout the book is that underpinning all our considerations, with regard to areas associated with problem solving, is having this clear view of the processes involved. Therefore, having decided to make this journey (and we set out the importance of considering this journey in Chapter 1), we started with a consideration of what is involved in problem solving. We were then able to delve in even greater depth in Chapters 3 and 4 into the importance, firstly of representing problems, and then the more encompassing process of reasoning and thinking with problems. Along the way, we took in different problem types, the issue of prior knowledge in problem solving, and the importance of reflection and metacognition, as well attempting to define processes such as 'representing' and 'thinking'.

Having made this initial part of the journey, the clarification of the problem-solving process allowed us to link to other related areas. Firstly, we were able to clarify why problem solving is associated so strongly with creativity in mathematics. Once again, we took in related issues such as problem posing. Another connected route that we took was trying to establish how we can assess problem posing. And indeed, both this issue of assessment and also the idea of creativity, in particular problem posing, led us to the next stage of the journey where we considered a variety of so-called open approaches in mathematics. Here, we took in approaches such as investigations, mathematical modelling, and the realistic mathematics education approach to the teaching and learning of mathematics. This then lead naturally to the final stage of our journey, and a consideration of why problem solving and other open approaches are considered to enrich and engage children in the subject of mathematics.

In using the metaphor of a journey to describe our progress through these ideas associated with problem solving, we may have perhaps failed to do justice to the interconnected nature of these ideas. Yes, our starting point was this clarification of what we mean by and what is involved in problem solving. Subsequently, however, what we hope to have achieved is to show how the other ideas are all interlinked – understanding one idea throws light on another idea associated with problem solving. Regardless of whether the metaphor of a journey is appropriate or not, we hope you have enjoyed this journey through understanding and enriching problem solving, that it has informed your reflections on classroom practice in your school and that, in the future, it will in some way positively impact on the mathematical experiences of children that you work with. We look forward to hearing from readers with regard to how appropriate the ideas in this book are for your practice in schools. As Richard Feynman alluded to in the introduction, the ideas in this book are simply the starting points for all our further reflections, to support us in our journey of refining practice. Once again, we hope you have enjoyed making this initial journey, and good luck in your future travels.

References

Askew, M (1996) 'Using and applying mathematics' in schools: reading the texts, in Johnson, D C, & Millett, A (eds) *Implementing the Mathematics National Curriculum* (pp 99–112). London: Paul Chapman Publishing Ltd

Balka, D S (1974) Creative ability in mathematics. *Arithmetic Teacher*, 21: 633–636

Barmby, P, Bilsborough, L, Harries, T, & Higgins, S (2009) *Primary mathematics: teaching for understanding*. Buckingham: Open University Press

Bautista, D, Mitchelmore, M, & Mulligan, J (2009) Factors influencing Filipino children's solutions to addition and subtraction word problems. *Educational Psychology*, 29(6): 729–745

Beghetto, R A (2007) Does creativity have a place in classroom discussions? Teachers' response preferences. *Thinking Skills and Creativity*, 2(1): 1–9

Blum, W, & Niss, M (1991) Applied mathematical problem solving, modelling, applications, and links to other subjects: state, trends and issues in mathematics instruction. *Educational studies in mathematics*, 22(1): 37–68

Boaler, J (2001) Mathematical modelling and new theories of learning. *Teaching Mathematics and its Applications*, 20(3): 121–127

Boden, M A (2004) *The creative mind – myths and mechanisms*. London: Routledge

Bolden, D S, Harries, A V, & Newton, D P (2010) Pre-service primary teachers' conceptions of creativity in mathematics. *Educational Studies in Mathematics*, 73(2): 143–157

Bolden, D S. & Newton, L D (2008) Primary teachers' epistemological beliefs: some perceived barriers to investigative teaching in primary mathematics. *Educational Studies*, 34(5): 419–432

Bourke, S, & Stacey, K (1988) Assessing problem solving in mathematics: some variables related to student performance. *The Australian Educational Researcher*, 15(1): 73–83

Brune, I (1953) Language in Mathematics, in Fehr, H F (ed) *The Learning of Mathematics: Its Theory and Practice*. Washington, DC: National Council of Teachers of Mathematics

Burkart, H, & Bell, A (2007) Problem solving in the United Kingdom. *ZDM*, 39: 395–405

Burton, L (1984) *Thinking things through: problem solving in mathematics*. Oxford: Blackwell

Burton, L (1998) The practices of mathematicians: what do they tell us about coming to know mathematics? *Educational Studies in Mathematics*, 37(2): 121–143

Carruthers, E, & Worthington, M (2005) Making sense of mathematical graphics: the development of understanding abstract symbolism. *European Childhood Research Journal*, 13(1): 57–79

Child, D (2004) *Psychology and the teacher*. London: Continuum

Clarkson, P C (1991) Mathematics in a multilingual society, in Durkin, K & Shire, B (eds) *Language in mathematical education* (pp 237–246). Buckingham: Open University Press

Cockcroft, W H (1982) *Mathematics counts: report of the Committee of Inquiry into the Teaching of Mathematics in Schools under the chairmanship of Dr W H Cockcroft*. London: HMSO

Collis, K F, Romberg, T A, & Jurdak, M E (1986) A technique for assessing mathematical problem-solving ability. *Journal for Research in Mathematics Education*, 17(3): 206–221

Cooper, B (1994) Authentic testing in mathematics? The boundary between everyday and mathematical knowledge in national curriculum testing in English schools. *Assessment in Education: Principles, Policy & Practice*, 1(2): 143–166

Cooper, B, & Dunne, M (2000) *Assessing children's mathematical knowledge: social class, sex and problem solving*. Buckingham: Open University Press

Craft, A (2003) The limits of creativity in education: Dilemmas for the educator. *British Journal of Educational Studies*, 51(2): 113–127

Crano, W D, & Prislin, R (2006) Attitudes and persuasion. *Annu. Rev. Psychol.*, 57: 345–374

Cropley, A J (1992) *More ways than one: fostering creativity*. New Jersey: Ablex

Csíkos, C, Szitányi, J, & Kelemen, R (2012) The effects of using drawings in developing young children's mathematical word problem solving: A design experiment with third-grade Hungarian students. *Educational Studies in Mathematics*, 81(1): 47–65

Csikszentmihalyi, M (1996) *Creativity: flow and the psychology of discovery and invention*. New York: Harper Collins

Davies, D, Howe, A, Rogers, M, & Fasciato, M (2004) How do trainee primary teachers understand creativity? In Norman, E, Spendlove, D, Graver, P & Mitchell, A (eds) *Creativity and innovation – DATA International Research Conference, DATA, Wellesbourne*. Project website: Retrieved April 3, 2014, from https://dspace.lboro.ac.uk/dspace-jspui/handle/2134/2865

Davis, R B (1984) *Learning mathematics: the cognitive science approach to mathematics education*. Norwood, NJ: Ablex Publishing Corporation

DCSF (2008) *Independent review of mathematics teaching in early years settings and primary schools*. London: DCSF

DCSF (2009) *Independent review of the primary curriculum*. London: DCSF

DfE (2013) *Mathematics programmes of study: key stages 1 and 2 – National curriculum in England*. London: DfE

DfEE (1999a) *The national curriculum handbook for primary teachers in England*. London: DfEE

DfEE (1999b) *The national numeracy strategy: Framework for teaching*. London: DfEE

DfEE & QCA (1999) *The National Curriculum for England – Mathematics*. London: DfEE & QCA

DfES (1989) *The national curriculum (England & Wales)*. London: DfES

DfES (2000) *Mathematical challenges for able pupils in Key Stages 1 and 2*. London: DfES

DfES (2003) *Excellence and enjoyment: a strategy for primary schools*. London: DfES

DfES (2004) *Problem solving: A CPD pack to support the learning and teaching of mathematical problem solving*. Norwich: DfES Publications

DfES (2006a) *Primary national strategy: Primary framework for literacy and mathematics*. London: DfES

DfES (2006b) *Reviewing the primary framework for mathematics guidance paper: Using and applying mathematics* London: DfES

DfES/DCMS (2006) *Nurturing Creativity in Young People*. London: DfES/DCMS

Dickinson, P, & Eade, F (2005) Trialling realistic mathematics education (RME) in English secondary schools. *Proceedings of the British Society for Research into Learning Mathematics*, 25(3)

Dickinson, P, Hough, S, Searle, J, & Barmby, P (2011) Evaluating the impact of a Realistic Mathematics Education project in secondary schools. *Proceedings of the British Society for Research into Learning Mathematics*, 31(3)

Durkin, K & Shire, B (1991) Lexical ambiguity in mathematical contexts, in Durkin, K & Shire, B (eds) *Language in mathematical education* (pp 71–84). Buckingham: Open University Press

Duval, R (1999) Representation, vision and visualization: Cognitive functions in mathematical thinking, in Hitt, F & Santos, M (eds) *Proceedings of the Twenty-first Annual Meeting of the North American Chapter of the International Group for the Psychology of Mathematics Education* (pp 3–26). Columbus, Ohio: ERIC Clearinghouse for Science, Mathematics, and Environmental Education

Ellerton, N F & Clarkson, P C (1996) Language factors in mathematics teaching and learning, in Bishop, A J, Clements, K, Keitel, C, Kilpatrick, J, Laborde, C (eds) *International handbook of mathematics education* (pp 987–1034). Dordrecht: Kluer Academic Publishers

English, L D, & Watters, J J (2005) Mathematical modelling in the early school years. *Mathematics Education Research Journal*, 16(3): 58–79

Feng, W Y (2006) Conceptions of Mathematics Enrichment. *Paper presented at BERA conference, Warwick, September 2006*

Flevares, L M, & Perry, M (2001) How many do you see? The use of nonspoken representations in first-grade mathematics lessons. *Journal of Educational Psychology*, 93(2): 330–345

Fredericks, J A, Blumenfeld, P C, & Paris, A H (2004) School engagement: Potential of the concept, state of the evidence. *Review of Educational Research*, 74(1): 59–109

Guilford, I P (1967) Creativity: Yesterday, today, and tomorrow. *The Journal of Creative Behaviour*, 1: 3–14

Gravemeijer, K (1994) Educational development and developmental research in mathematics education. *Journal for Research in Mathematics Education*, 25(5): 443–471

Gravemeijer, K (1999) How emergent models may foster the constitution of formal mathematics. *Mathematical Thinking and Learning*, 1(2): 155–177

Gregory, R L (2009) *Seeing through illusions*. Oxford: Oxford University Press

Gruber, H E, & Wallace, D B (2000) The case study method and evolving systems approach for understanding unique creative people at work, in Sternberg, R J (ed) *Handbook of Creativity* (pp 93–115). Cambridge: Cambridge University Press

Hadamard, J (1954) *The Psychology of invention in the mathematical field*. New York: Dover Publications

Haylock, D (1987) A framework for assessing mathematical creativity in schoolchildren. *Educational Studies in Mathematics*, 18(1): 59–74

Haylock, D (1997) Recognising mathematical creativity in schoolchildren. *International Journal on Mathematical Education*, 29(3): 68–74

Hiebert, J, Carpenter, T P, Fennema, E, Fuson, K, Human, P, Murray, H, Olivier, A, & Wearne, D (1996) Problem solving as a basis for reform in curriculum and instruction: the case of mathematics. *Educational Researcher*, 25(4) 12–21

Holyoak, K J, & Morrison, R G (2005) Thinking and reasoning: a reader's guide, in Holyoak, K J & Morrison, R G (eds) *The Cambridge handbook of thinking and reasoning* (pp 1–9). New York: Cambridge University Press

Hoyles, C, Sutherland, R & Healy, L (1991) Children talking in computer environments: New insights into the role of discussion in mathematics learning, in Durkin, K & Shire, B (eds) *Language in mathematical education* (pp 162–176). Buckingham: Open University Press

Jensen, T (2007) Assessing mathematical modeling competencies, in Haines, C, Galbraith, P, Blum, W & Khan, S (eds) *Mathematical modeling (ICTMA 12): Education, engineering and economics* (pp 141–148). Chichester: Horwood

Johnson-Laird, P N (1983) *Mental models: Towards a cognitive science of language, inference, and consciousness*. Cambridge: Cambridge University Press

Johnson-Laird, P N (2005) Mental models and thought, in Holyoak, K J, & Morrison, R G (eds) *The Cambridge handbook of thinking and reasoning* (pp 185–208). New York: Cambridge University Press

Jones, L (2003) The Problem with Problem Solving, in Thompson, I (ed) *Enhancing Primary Mathematics Teaching* (pp 86–98). Maidenhead: Open University Press

Joseph, G G (1991) *The crest of the peacock: non-European roots of mathematics*. London: Penguin Books

Kahney, H (1993) *Problem solving: current issues*. Maidenhead: Open University Press

Kaput, J (1985) Representation and problem solving: methodological issues related to the modelling, in Silver, E (ed), *Teaching and learning mathematical problem solving: multiple research perspectives* (pp 381–398). Hillsdale, NJ: Lawrence Erlbaum Associates

Kaput, J J (1991) Notations and representations as mediators of constructive processes, in von Glasersfeld, E (ed) *Radical constructivism in mathematics education* (pp 53–74). Dordrecht: Kluwer

Kennedy, M (2005) *Inside teaching: how classroom life undermines reform*. Cambridge, MA: Harvard University Press

Kong, Q-P, Wong, N-Y, & Lam, C-C (2003) Student engagement in mathematics: development of instrument and validation of construct. *Mathematics Education Research Journal*, 15(1): 4–21

Koshy, V (2003) Nurturing mathematical promise, in Thompson, I (ed) *Enhancing primary mathematics teaching* (pp 136–150). Milton Keynes: Open University Press

Krutetskii, V A (1976) *The psychology of mathematical abilities in school children*. Chicago: The University of Chicago Press

Kwon, O H, Park, J S & Park, J S (2006) Cultivating divergent thinking in mathematics through an open-ended approach. *Asia-Pacific Education Review*, 7(1): 51–61

Lee, K S, Hwang, D J, & Seo, J J (2003) A development of the test for mathematical creative problem solving ability. *Journal of The Korea Society of Mathematical Education*, 7: 163–189

Leikin, R, Berman, R, & Koichu, B (eds) (2009) *Creativity in mathematics and the education of gifted students*. Rotterdam: Sense Publishers

Lesh, R (1981) Applied mathematical problem solving. *Educational Studies in Mathematics*, 12(2): 235–264

Lesh, R & Doerr, H M (2003) Foundations of models and modeling perspectives on mathematics teaching, learning, and problem solving, in Lesh, R & Doerr, H (eds) *Beyond constructivism: Models and modeling perspectives on mathematics problem solving, learning, and teaching* (pp 3–33). Mahwah, NJ: Lawrence Erlbaum Associates Inc

Makel, M C (2009) Help us creativity researchers, you're our only hope. *Psychology of Aesthetics, Creativity and the Arts*, 3: 38–42

Mann, E L (2006) Creativity: the essence of mathematics. *Journal for the Education of the Gifted*, 30(2): 236–260

Mason, J, Burton, L, & Stacey, K (1985) *Thinking mathematically*. Wokingham: Addison-Wesley Publishing Company

Mayer, R E (1992) *Thinking, problem solving, cognition*. WH Freeman/Times Books/Henry Holt & Co

Meece, J L, Blumenfeld, P C & Hoyle, R H (1988) Students' goal orientations and cognitive engagement in classroom activities. *Journal of Educational Psychology*, 80(4): 514–523

Mosely, D, Baumfield, V, Elliott, J, Gregson, M, Higgins, S, Miller, J, & Newton, D P (2005) *Frameworks for thinking: a handbook for teaching and learning*. Cambridge: Cambridge University Press

Munns, G, & Woodward, H (2006) Student engagement and student self-assessment: the REAL framework. *Assessment in Education*, 13(2): 193–213

Murphy, C (2011) Comparing the use of the empty number line in England and the Netherlands. *British Educational Research Journal*, 37(1): 147–161

NACCCE (1999) *All our futures: creativity, culture and education*. London, DfEE

Newmann, F M, Wehlage, G G, & Lamborn, S D (1992) The significance and sources of student engagement, in Newmann, F M (ed) *Student engagement and achievement in American secondary school* (pp 11–39). New York: Teachers College Press

Newton, L D (2012) *Creativity for a new curriculum: 5–11*. Routledge: London

Nicholson, A R (1977) Mathematics and language. *Mathematics in School*, 6(5) 32–34

Nickerson, R S (1994) The teaching of thinking and problem solving, in Sternberg, R J (ed) *Thinking and problem solving* (pp 409–449). London: Academic Press

Ofsted (2008) *Mathematics: Understanding the score. Improving practice in mathematics teaching at primary level*. London: Ofsted

Ofsted (2009) *Expecting the Unexpected: Developing Creativity in Primary and Secondary Schools*. London: Ofsted

Ofsted (2013) *Promoting improvement in Initial Teacher Education (ITE): primary mathematics (Ofsted Ref: 20130016)*. Retrieved January 15, 2014, from http://www.ofsted.gov.uk/resources/promoting-improvement-initial-teacher-education-ite-primary-mathematics

Orton, A (2004) *Learning mathematics (3rd Edition)*. London: Continuum

Orton, A & Frobisher, L (1996) *Insights into teaching mathematics*. London: Cassell

Pantziara, M, Gagatsis, A, & Elia, I (2009) Using diagrams as tools for the solution of non-routine mathematical problems. *Educational Studies in Mathematics*, 72(1): 39–60

Pape, S J, & Tchoshanov, M A (2001) The role of representation(s) in developing mathematical understanding. *Theory into Practice*, 40(2): 118–127

Park, S-Y (2005) Student engagement and classroom variables in improving mathematics achievement. *Asia-Pacific Education Review*, 6(1): 87–97

Pehkonen, E (1997) The state-of-art in mathematical creativity. *ZDM*, 29(3): 63–67

Peterson, P L, & Fennema, E (1985) Effective teaching, student engagement in classroom activities, and sex-related differences in learning mathematics. *American Educational Research Journal*, 22(3): 309–335

Piggott, J (2004) Mathematical enrichment: what is it and who is it for? *Paper presented at BERA conference, Manchester, September 2004*

Polya, G (1957) *How to solve it: A new aspect of mathematical method*. New York: Doubleday Anchor Books

Polya, G (1981) *Mathematical discovery*. Chichester: John Wiley

Ponte, J (2001) Investigating in mathematics and in learning to teach mathematics. In Lin, F L & Cooney, T J (eds) *Making sense of mathematics teacher education* (pp 53–72). Dordrecht: Kluwer

Ponte, J P (2007) Investigations and explorations in the mathematics classroom. *ZDM*, 39(5): 419–430

Pretz, J E, Naples, A J & Sternberg, R J (2003) Recognizing, defining, and representing problems, in Davidson, J E & Sternberg, R J (eds) *The psychology of problem solving* (pp 3–30). Cambridge: Cambridge University Press

Redmond, T, Brown, R, Sheehy, J & Kanasa, H (2012) Exploring Student Reflective Practice during a Mathematical Modelling Challenge, in *Mathematics education: Expanding horizons. Proceedings of the 35th Annual Conference of the Mathematics Education Research Group of Australasia (MERGA)*, Singapore (Vol. 2, pp 642–649)

Sangster, M (2012) The rise and fall of an investigative approach to mathematics in primary education. *Proceedings of the British Society for Research into Learning Mathematics*, 32(1)

Santos, S, & Barmby, P (2010) Enrichment and engagement in mathematics. *Paper presented at the 7th British Conference in Mathematics Education, University of Manchester*

Santos-Trigo, M (2007) Mathematical problem solving: an evolving research and practice domain. *ZDM*, 39(5): 523–536

Schoenfeld, A H (1992) Learning to think mathematically: Problem solving, metacognition, and sense-making in mathematics, in Grouws, D A (ed) *Handbook of research on mathematics teaching and learning* (pp. 334–370). New York: MacMillan

Sheffield, L J (1999) The development of mathematically promising students in the United States. *Mathematics in School*, 28(3): 15–18

Sheffield, L J (2009) Developing mathematical creativity: questions may be the answer, in Leikin, R, Berman, A & Koichu B (eds) *Creativity in mathematics and the education of gifted students* (pp 87–100). Rotterdam: Sense Publishers

Silver, E A (1994) On mathematical problem posing. *For the learning of mathematics*, 14(1): 19–28

Silver, E A (1997) Fostering creativity through instruction rich in mathematical problem solving and problem posing. *ZDM*, 29(3): 75–80

Silver, E A (2013) Problem-posing research in mathematics education: looking back, looking around, and looking ahead. *Educational Studies in Mathematics*, 83(1): 157–162

Skemp, R R (1989) *Mathematics in the primary school*. London: Routledge

Skiba, T, Tan, M, Sternberg, R J & Grigorenko, E L (2010) Roads not taken, new roads to take: looking for creativity in the classroom, In Beghetto, R A & Kaufman, J C (eds) *Nurturing Creativity in the Classroom* (pp 252–269). New York: Cambridge University Press

Sriraman, B (2005) Are giftedness and creativity synonyms in mathematics? *The Journal of Secondary Gifted Education*, 27(1): 20–36

Sriraman, B (ed) (2008) *Creativity, giftedness, and talent development in mathematics*. Charlotte: Information Age Publishing, Inc

Sternberg, R J (ed) (1988) *The nature of creativity: contemporary psychological perspectives*. New York: Cambridge University Press

Straker, A (1999) The National Numeracy Project: 1996–1999, in Thompson, I (ed) *Issues in Teaching Numeracy in Primary Schools* (pp 39–48). Buckingham: Open University Press

Szetela, W (1987) The problem of evaluation in problem solving: can we find solutions? *The Arithmetic Teacher*, November, 36–41

Tanner, H & Jones, S (2002) Assessing children's mathematical thinking in practical modelling situations. *Teaching Mathematics and its Applications*, 21(4): 145–159

Threlfall, J (2010) The 'gifted and talented', in Thompson, I (ed) *Issues in teaching numeracy in primary schools (2nd edition)* (pp 235–247). Buckingham: Open University Press

Toh, T L, Quek, K S, Leong, Y H, Dindyal, J, & Tay, E G (2009) Assessment in a problem solving curriculum, in Hunter, R, Bicknell, B & Burgess, T (eds) *Crossing divides: proceedings of the 32nd annual conference of the Mathematics Education Research Group of Australasia (Vol. 1)* (pp 686–690). Palmerston North, NZ: MERGA

Torrance, E P (1974) *Torrance tests of creative thinking*. Bensenville: Scholastic Testing Service

Treffers, A, & Beishuizen, M (1999) Realistic mathematics education in the Netherlands, in Thompson, I (ed) *Issues in teaching numeracy in primary schools* (pp 27–38) Buckingham: Open University Press

Treffinger, D J, Young, G C, Selby, E C & Shepardson, C A (2002) *Assessing creativity*. Storrs, CT: The National Research Center on the Gifted and Talented

Van den Heuvel-Panhuizen, M (1998) Realistic Mathematics Education as work in progress, In Lin, F L (ed) *Common sense in mathematics education: proceedings of 2001 the Netherlands and Taiwan conference on mathematics education* (pp 1–43). Taipei, Taiwan, 19–23 November 2001

Van den Heuvel-Panhuizen, M (2003) The didactical use of models in realistic mathematics education: an example from a longitudinal trajectory on percentage. *Educational Studies in Mathematics*, 54(1): 9–35

Verschaffel, L, De Corte, E, & Lasure, S (1994) Realistic considerations in mathematical modeling of school arithmetic word problems. *Learning and Instruction, 4(4):* 273–294

Waring, S (2000) *Can you prove it?: Developing concepts of proof in primary and secondary schools.* Leicester: Mathematical Association

Watts, M (1991) *The science of problem-solving.* London: Cassell

Weisberg, R W (1988) Problem solving and creativity, in Sternberg, R J (ed) *The nature of creativity* (pp 148–176). Cambridge: Cambridge University Press

Wood, D (1998) *How children think and learn: the social contexts of cognitive development.* Oxford: Blackwell Publishing

Woolfolk, A, Hughes, M & Walkup, V (2008) *Psychology in Education.* London: Pearson Longman

Worthington, M & Carruthers, E (2003) *Children's mathematics: making marks, making meaning.* London: Paul Chapman

Index